With fondness
to Yvonne

T. J Smith
Jun 08

Kinship
and the Dark Side of Man

*The Secrets of How Life Works
and Where We Go Wrong*

Theodore J. Smith, M.D. and Kim Smith, M.D.

Order this book online at www.trafford.com/05-2769
or email orders@trafford.com

Most Trafford titles are also available at major online book retailers.

Note for Librarians: A cataloguing record for this book is available from Library
and Archives Canada at www.collectionscanada.ca/amicus/index-e.html

Printed in Victoria, BC, Canada.

ISBN: 978-1-4120-7871-9

*We at Trafford believe that it is the responsibility of us all, as both individuals
and corporations, to make choices that are environmentally and socially sound.
You, in turn, are supporting this responsible conduct each time you purchase a
Trafford book, or make use of our publishing services. To find out how you are
helping, please visit www.trafford.com/responsiblepublishing.html*

*Our mission is to efficiently provide the world's finest, most comprehensive
book publishing service, enabling every author to experience success.
To find out how to publish your book, your way, and have it available
worldwide, visit us online at www.trafford.com/10510*

 www.trafford.com

North America & international
toll-free: 1 888 232 4444 (USA & Canada)
phone: 250 383 6864 ♦ fax: 250 383 6804 ♦ email: info@trafford.com

The United Kingdom & Europe
phone: +44 (0)1865 722 113 ♦ local rate: 0845 230 9601
facsimile: +44 (0)1865 722 868 ♦ email: info.uk@trafford.com

10 9 8 7 6 5 4 3 2 1

Dedication

This book is dedicated to the spirit of inquiry that led us to the knowledge of behavior and our lifework of using that knowledge to help ourselves and others live the full human potential.

Acknowledgements

We are profoundly grateful to our thousands of patients for what they have taught us. We are also indebted to Damion Kirk for his encouragement and seminal ideas, to Rob Robb for his living example, and to Ryen West for her patient and skillful editing.

Contents

Dedication iii

Acknowledgements v

Contents vii

Preface xi

Introduction 1

Kinship 5

Beliefs 13

The Basic Nature of Emotional Development 21

Developing Attitudes 31

Attitude is Age Related 39

Emotional Development as Reflected in Attitude 43

Ultimate Emotional Development 51

Correlation of Fear and Defense 59

Affirmation of an Infant 73

Goals 77

Intuition 81

Intuition & Attitude 91

Managing Emotional Energy 97

Power..107

Victim 117

Stifling Enthusiasm and Spontaneity 121

Central Nervous System and Our Dark Side............129

Behavior, DNA, and Beliefs................................141

Emotional Responses..147

Serious Emotional Disorders..............................151

Behavioral Aspects of Psychiatric Problems............157

    Antisocial Personality, ...157
    Including the Criminal Mind Set.............................157
    Borderline Personality 159
    Depression...161
    Posttraumatic Stress Disorder.............................165

Domination Contest 169

Anger and Dependence 177

Obesity and Shame 179

Permutations of Anger 189

Further Permutations of Anger 199

Anger Summary...207

The Anger Game 209

Understanding Classroom Gunfire 213

Truth and Reality...227

Management of Feelings 233

Changing Our Beliefs................................253

More on Changing Our Belief Systems.....................259

Understanding the Terrorist's Behavior 263

The Controlled Mind 277

Brainwashing.....................................279

Frankness and Reality...............................287

Case History—Jill 291

Case History—William 301

Fear Spoils the Quality of Life 309

Green-Spotted Yellow-Bellied Alligator...................315

Augmentation of Imagery.............................325

Remaking Infantile Attitudes 337

Good and Evil.....................................349

Our Continuous Conversation 357

The Origin of Thought..............................361

Our True Identity 365

Summation: Be True to Thyself.........................371

Epilogue...375

Appendices 393

   a. The Technique of Directed Age Reenactment.............. 393
   b. Exercise to Reestablish Individuality 403
   c. Group Anger Management: an Outline................ 409
   d. Twelve Steps for Growth 425

Preface

Our subconscious minds forget nothing. If we did forget, fear would be nonexistent. The fact that fear does exist signifies that, deep down, we do remember and consequently have built-in conjoint defense reactions.

Although we can no longer consciously recall all the highly emotional experiences of our lives, these experiences are precise impressions in our subconscious minds. Special traumatic incidents recorded in our subconscious minds are more prominent and easier to defensively reenact than purely factual incidents, which are less deeply etched and more difficult to recall. Often, the repetition of minor traumatic incidents can also easily provoke the reenactment of defensive reactions.

Both this book and Ted's previous book, *Full Share*, represent analyses of accumulated data acquired from working with patients for over fifty years for Ted and twenty-five years for Kim. The process is similar to geologists analyzing a rock brought back from the moon to get some understanding of how the rock formed.

Full Share deals extensively with the origins of fear and emotional arrests acquired between the ages of three and six. In this book, we focus on personality arrests generated in infants from birth to the age of three. The formation of protective reactions causes the formation of age related attitudes that direct our behavior. Our basic beliefs and attitudes, coupled with our minds' expectations, are what determine our emotions.

In this book, we describe the formation of beliefs and their resistance to revision. A good share of our severe social problems, including criminality, drug addiction, professional homelessness, and domestic violence, are due to attitudes from personality arrests acquired during infancy. As a physician who specializes in internal medicine, Ted's chief interest is in diagnosis and analysis, that is, understanding the cause and formation of each intellectual and emotional process. Kim, specializing in emergency medicine, is primarily interested in managing life's challenges.

Half of all human disease conditions are developed as automatic self-protections that people in infancy and childhood need in order to maintain their individualities and physical survival. These self-protections are all generated by fear. Except in cases of some long term or continuing exposure to stress, these defense reactions should be transitory. However, if we learn behaviors that save our lives and our individualities, these defense reactions will be very resistant to change or to even slight modification. All sustained defenses, to remain active or in reserve readiness, take a stressful toll on our bodies' machinery.

The ultimate realization concerning relationships is that all discomforts, including resentments, fears, and disappointments, are our own contributions and projections, stemming from our own emotional arrests, and in reality, the only relationship one can have is the one with one's self. All defenses and resistances are developed to protect our individualities, but inadvertently cause arrests in our emotional maturity. These developmental blocks keep us from living and loving in the NOW.

The revision or treatment of our emotional responses, first and foremost, requires that we accept that we are solely responsible for any disharmonies that arise, and that we, alone, have the power to improve.

Introduction

In our modern society, in spite of stress, most of us will live longer than our parents. However, we have increasingly realized that quality of life is the true goal, and if we have been delayed or misdirected, this book will allow us to identify the salient factors that comprise the quality, and will offer us a guide towards reaching that goal. Two important aspects of quality of life are these: accepting ourselves fully for all that we are, and successfully enjoying our interpersonal relationships. Even if we are recluses, the one important factor in our fulfillment will be how fully we accept ourselves.

Exploring this line of thought, we start by examining the everyday encounters that impact our lives, beginning with the obvious common denominator, human behavior. All behaviors are the products of our own individual attitudes, and those of the people with whom we interact. The traits of individuals range widely, but in general, they are amazingly constant within each of us. This consistency is defined by the personal attitudes that govern us. Our attitudes define our states of mind. Attitudes and choices determine our expectations. All of us have our own unique expectations which, in turn, almost entirely determine our emotions. For example, if we believe that imprecise driving is always meant to be personally insulting, and someone cuts us off on the freeway, we become angry. But who knows what was going on in the other driver's mind? He may have been momentarily distracted by a thought of something he had forgotten to do that day, and didn't mean to be rude. Yet our anger arises because of our beliefs about what certain things mean.

Our expectations can be wildly unrealistic when they are based on ideas of what we want ourselves to be rather than what we feel ourselves to be in actuality. Much of our energy is wasted in presenting ourselves as we would like ourselves to be. However, there is no stress when our expectations are based on realistic attitudes about ourselves. This book will examine the formation and revision of subconscious beliefs, which, taken together, determine our attitudes and emotions.

The human mind is the gatekeeper that controls our exposure to all new and additional information that could strengthen or revise our beliefs. It is ironic that our most important attitudes about our self-worth, self-images, and self-esteem are those we learn in infancy, when our brains are in a rudimentary state of development, and we lack perspective. Our attitudes toward life, acquired in infancy, will determine its quality permanently, unless specific steps are taken to revise these beliefs and attitudes. It is never too late in life to begin this revision, for the reward is a greatly enhanced enjoyment of every moment.

Kinship

When we are born, we are immature in many ways, and we have urgent and sustained dependency needs. The obvious needs are physical, such as protection, air, water, and nutrition, and must be fulfilled if we are to become substantially strong and healthy. Equally important is the need for supporting, loving environments, affording us the opportunity for emotional growth and development. Emotionally, we require acceptance. Acceptance includes the component of love, but love has many dictionary meanings—twenty-two of them—and each person has his own understanding of what love is. But acceptance has a more commonly agreed upon connotation. For every mammal in an immature state, including human children, acceptance means life, while rejection means death.

We have been very successful in modern times at providing physical support and protection for human infants, enabling them to mature to healthy adults. In contrast, our children's need for emotional and nurturing acceptance as separate but equal individuals is widely ignored or is misunderstood. The essential need for emotional nurturing, the vital ingredient for a full future life, is vastly underestimated. Acceptance and esteem are at the center of meaningful, intimate, interpersonal relationships. *Love* that does not have acceptance as its main ingredient will not be meaningful to us as infants. At birth, acceptance is entirely one sided and must come from our caretakers. We must experience the feeling of acceptance before we can emulate it.

As parents, we should have esteem for our children's separate individualities, the potentials of which are encoded in their DNA. Love for our babies, without esteem for their separate and equal individualities, will create emotionally dysfunctional adults. Ideally, we must completely trust that our children already have all the important skills and qualities embedded in their genes, and that they will unfold them at the proper times, without any coaching or instruction from us.

In the beginning, acceptance must come from without. Our children emulate their caretakers' acceptance or lack of acceptance of them as they adopt feelings of self-worth or lack of self-worth as their fixed and usually permanent attitudes for the rest of their lives. As adults, full acceptance of ourselves, and therefore of others, is essential for our ultimate attainment of quality of life.

The highest emotional development at maturity is achieved when we can and will totally accept ourselves as we are. This is reality, enlightenment, or becoming one with the Buddha. This does not mean that we are better than anyone else, for at maturity, we no longer make comparisons of ourselves with others. The culmination of our ultimate search is to appreciate and develop as much as we can of all the potential with which we are endowed. Our lives are not long enough to accomplish all of this, but our fulfillment will be ever increasing as our search and development continues.

Our challenge begins at birth. By nature's design, we start out with self-acceptance, because, at the time of our birth, nobody else in the world matters to us.

Initially, because we are nearly helpless, our feelings of importance, individuality, and self-respect must be recognized and continued from outside ourselves.

Beginning at birth, emotional acceptance is the sole province of our parents. Throughout childhood, but more especially, during the first thirty-six months, there are no more important learning experiences than those taught by example through modeling. We mimic our parents. During our first three years, it is very difficult to develop any more esteem for ourselves than the esteem that one parent holds and practices toward the other.

Our parents had only the tools of interpersonal relationship and teaching that were passed down to them from their parents. Kinship brings forth and exposes their handicaps, as exemplified by their failings to accept each other and themselves. Our parents' deficiencies become evident when they are more upset and angry with us and our siblings than they are with their friends and acquaintances, and also when they are angry at themselves, as evidenced by their behaving in any way that would indicate that they feel themselves to be undeserving. The opposite of feeling undeserving is not arrogance or aggression, but self-assurance that can only come from within, through self-acceptance.

Except by providing examples, our parents can do very little during our first three years that could possibly be helpful. Some of the most emotionally damaging and stifling influences in our young lives are the instructions inflicted on us long before our nervous systems are mature enough to process such training. Before our brains are physiologically ready, demanding instructions for learning performance tricks that our parents attempt to inflict on us can be accomplished only at the lifelong expense of blocking some of our own potential creative development. By all measures, our chief learning as infants is through intimate exposure to the feelings and behavior of our parents by their projected acceptance, speech, habits, customs, and attitudes. Cardinal is our parents' esteem for us as separate individuals; this expression alone is the major factor that either limits or encourages us to develop a lifelong acceptance of ourselves.

When we "take it out" on our families and those who are, or should be, close to us emotionally, this abuse is the sign that we have limited assessments of our own self-worth. So common is this behavior, that forty years ago the very popular quartet, the Mills Brothers, popularized and immortalized an extraordinary song, featuring the words, "We always hurt the one we love, the one we shouldn't hurt at all, and if I broke your heart last night, it's because I love you most of all." Such a declaration is evidence of emotional regression and reenactment of unfulfilled, ancient, dependency needs. That emotional part of us is still in a needy, infantile stage. The closer the kinship, the deeper is the hurt, because our expectations are so much greater. Also, we will more strongly express and proclaim our anger at family members for the perceived rejection—not having received the support and succor we have always needed, but have not received since birth. This behavior follows the general rule that we see and comprehend first in others those qualities or traits that we lack or despise in ourselves.

The problem is that we consider our spouses and children to be *ours,* or parts of us, and we don't like ourselves. In essence, we are not being any harder in our treatment of them than we are on ourselves when we indulge in self-castigation. Our anger is rekindled and demonstrates evidence that our crucial, sought-after dependency need fulfillment is being ignored by our loved ones. They are expecting us to take care of them, when we are the tender ones who need the care.

Rather than supporting us, they are demanding that we satisfy their unrealistic expectations. We are tuned into ourselves, with our own unsatisfied dependency needs, rather than actively tuned into them and their required attention for reassurance in their own immature states. The worker who toils solely for anticipated compensation could be compared to a father whose "service" is done for anticipated love in return.

Ideally, our lives' work consists of those tasks that we thoroughly enjoy, and thereby, our activities fulfill our creative spirits. Consequently, we receive compensation adequate for our needs. Simply working to get a wage can be stultifying, and working to get love from another person or beast is putting emphasis at the wrong end. Esteem is hard to generate, for it should be spontaneous. As a natural principle, we will warmly regard and even love whoever or whatever accepts us as we are.

Clearly, this acceptance is not something we can work to get. However, we can work on ourselves to accord ourselves acceptance, and, in fact, we must. If acceptance is not fully extended to us in childhood, as it should be, especially in our first three years, then we are left with the realization that we are the only ones who can accept us for ourselves alone. We can beg, plead, and attempt to purchase someone to accept us, but the extending of acceptance is an entirely personal decision, and it is determined and limited by each person's own experience and sense of security. When we find ourselves able to accept no one, even our children, it means only one thing—we cannot accept ourselves. Self-love is a fool's quest, but learning to accept ourselves will inevitability produce that passive self-love. In a sense, it is payment for the interest and effort we invest in ourselves for being ourselves as opposed to doing for ourselves. Kinship means that, for better or worse, attitudes are always shared in families, and the only life-supporting attitude is simple acceptance. In childrearing, this means acceptance without any instruction, based on full trust that our infants will surely find their own best ways, directed by their perfect genetic instructions.

Beliefs

Life can seem extraordinarily complex, and human behavior is varied and sometimes confusing. The complex behaviors we see in ourselves and in others all derive, however, from a simple system wherein our perceptions, and the emotions they generate, are all under the direct controlling influence of our unconscious beliefs. By beliefs, we mean not what we consciously believe our opinions to be, but rather those fundamental positions on self-worth, our positions in society, and innumerable other intricacies of human life which we hold unconsciously and steadfastly. Most of us have no idea what our true beliefs are. For example, if we ask people if money can buy happiness, they will most likely answer, "No," since we've all been taught that that's the correct answer. As a result, most of us do hold the belief that happiness cannot be bought. However, if we ask those same people, "Do you think you'd be happier if you made an extra $2,000 every month?" they may well say, "Yes." On the face of it then, they do believe that money can buy happiness, because they act in a manner consistent with that belief. This, incidentally, is one of the best ways to know what our own unconscious beliefs are; simply take a look at what we're doing. We will always behave consistently with our subconscious beliefs.

We have beliefs about absolutely everything. We have beliefs about fundamental things like our self-worth, the degree to which other people can be trusted, the joy we are allowed to experience from sharing ourselves with others, the amount of wealth we will allow in our lives, the amount of success we believe we deserve and will accept, and what our relationship behavior should be like. Also, we have beliefs about even minor things—which kind of food is good and which isn't; what kinds of streets are safe to walk on and which are not; with whom it is appropriate to start a conversation and with whom it is not. In short, every part of our lives is determined by our beliefs.

Occasionally, there are new situations that contain components for which we have not yet developed beliefs, and, in those situations, we feel confused and uncertain. However, we quickly form beliefs which, until more information comes along, are maintained as our operating deciding principles in that new area. The function of beliefs in human life is to simplify our lives and make them livable. If we had to decide everything every day, the strain on our intellects would be overwhelming. For example, if we got up in the morning and had to decide anew whether to take a bath or a shower and what temperature the water should be, where we were going to have breakfast, what kind of work we were going to go to that day and how we were going to get there, which route to take, which method of transportation to use and so on, every day would be an exhausting reinvention of our lives. Fortunately, human life is not constructed that way, and once we make decisions, we turn them over to our unconscious minds for execution.

The difficulty with this whole situation is that most of us are totally unaware of our most important beliefs, those governing our self-worth and our intimate relationships, and those particular decisions were made extremely early in life, before we had informed perspective. As a result, as this book will further elucidate, we often decided in a way that limits us severely and causes us unhappiness in our later lives.

The best way to think about beliefs is to compare them to computer programs, operating in the background until they are called upon. If we have computers, we know that there are many components of the operating system, of which we are not aware unless we open the system folder and explore, and all of these programs operate at the appropriate times when items that require them are presented. We can use computers without knowing about all of those small sub-programs, but computers would be useless without them. Such it is with human life. We have literally thousands of beliefs, some major, some very minor, and they determine how we will manage individual situations and perceptions. For example, if we believe that we are love-worthy and other people are love-worthy as well, then every day, we find people who stimulate our feelings of love, and we often find ourselves readily accepted to a deep degree by others, even strangers. This is because, based upon the belief that we are love-worthy, we automatically screen out evidence to the contrary and delete it, and we accept all evidence that is consistent with our beliefs. As a result, we notice every friendly face, every gesture of openness, every feeling of warmth emanating from other people during our day. We respond to these feelings and smile ourselves, gesture in ways that show openness and love, and radiate deep feelings of acceptance to which people respond readily. Conversely, if our fundamental beliefs from an early age, when we make these sorts of decisions, are that we are not worthy of love and very few other people are either, then our day looks completely different, even if we go to the same restaurants, interact with the same people, go to the same workplaces, and have the same clients or patients. Instead of the loving experiences of the previous case, we find that people seem distant and cold, and they seem this way because we systematically screen out any evidence to the contrary. We disregard any warm gestures and hone in on any aspects of behavior that imply reserve, distance, concern, trepidation, anger or rejection, and we may be experienced by other people as having cold demeanors, speech that does not invite reciprocation, gestures that do not convey openness, and emanations of rejection rather than warmth and acceptance. The result is that our day is filled with evidence to support our beliefs that people don't love us and we don't love them. Beliefs absolutely determine which perceptions we allow and which we delete.

There is always ample evidence to support whatever beliefs we may have. An interesting demonstration of this can be made by writing down the absolute facts of our lives. In other words, the places and dates of our births, the occupations of our parents, the years that we moved to different places, the schools we attended, the names of our friends; in other words, verifiable, objective facts about our personal histories. Then, using only these facts, we first write the stories of our lives from the points of view of those who are blessed by good fortune and have been helped by circumstance at all periods of their lives to have joy and fulfillment. Then, using the same facts, we tell stories of our lives from the points of view of those who are victims, who have cursed existences, doomed from the beginning to be filled with frustration and disappointment. What we find in this exercise is that the facts can be used to support opposite points of view, and this is the case with our everyday lives. We do not ever see what is truly around us or within us. We cannot. By nature, we can see only what we have decided to allow ourselves to see, and that will determine our emotions. If we believe that love is the norm, then we constantly have our feelings of love reinforced, with the smiles of passersby on the street, with the embraces of our coworkers, with the tenderness of our family members. Every day, our feelings of love, warmth, and joy are reinforced. However, if our beliefs are otherwise to begin with, then only evidence of the futility of life is allowed into our awareness. The only way the quality of our lives can be upgraded is to change the beliefs which are limiting our enjoyment. The changing of beliefs is a process requiring guidance and will be discussed in another section.

The Basic Nature of Emotional Development

The inherent drives in all human beings have an order of importance:

1. Stay alive and procreate.

2. Develop new defenses to contend with situational threats.

3. Mimic and adopt our caretakers' senses of respect and acceptance as they demonstrate their attitudes regarding themselves. This straight-across adoption of parental attitudes continues actively as long as we feel dependent on our caretakers for survival.

4. Accept ourselves.

5. Fulfill the human potentials encoded in our personal DNA.

We are utterly dependent on our caretakers when

we are born. Throughout infancy and then in childhood, we should be decreasingly dependent upon them for both physical and emotional support. Our caretakers' initial acceptance of us, physically, is paramount for life, and rejection is certain death. Physical acceptance is demonstrated by the supplying of food, warmth, and shelter. These essentials keep our bodies alive, and in our modern Western world, physical support, along with hygienic environments and immunizations, are increasingly available.

In infancy, we have little or no ability to evaluate anything. In order to remain alive within our families, we instinctively adopt familial and tribal attitudes as our own. However, these accretions of beliefs prove later to have been done at a high cost. The acquisition of attitudes from outside of us, rather than from the emotions in the templates of our personal DNA, causes reciprocal reductions in our senses of individual separateness. Tribal beliefs and attitudes are developed solely for the benefit and self-perpetuation of organized social orders and don't recognize individuals.

Except for survival itself, there is nothing more important in infancy than establishing our strong individual identities. During our first three years of life, our major mission is to develop the sense of separateness from our parents that will allow us the space to evolve our all-important self-images. This separation from our parents is necessary if we are to retain our trust in our own intuition and belief in ourselves. The degree to which we form these strong self-images will determine to what extent we will dare to accept ourselves as adults and receive inner guidance from our DNA. Our self-acceptance in turn will determine the degree to which we will accept our own children and all other people.

The imposition of parental and tribal attitudes forces arrests in our own maturing attitudes that, in turn, forever control our basic behavior. Long before logic and reason start to kick in, whenever we sense life-threats that trigger feelings of personal inadequacy, we form additional ongoing defenses. These defenses are founded on specific images of our separate vulnerabilities and cause us to automatically respond protectively by shutting down, avoiding, or getting clear of any anticipated recurrences of the dreaded initial threats. This phenomenon is necessary, for we must continue to be alive in order to have possible opportunities for subsequent emotional growth.

However, when these defenses are held intact and continued into adulthood, they are evidence that we remain insecure about ourselves. This logically leads us back to the fact that our feelings of security are proportional to the degree that we have accepted ourselves. Self-acceptance and belief in ourselves are essential to our development as entirely adequate, separate individuals.

During infancy, there are truly life threatening physical hazards, but there are also emotional, soul-threatening hazards emanating from other people in the form of rejection, mainly of our individualities. We reduce our self-esteem when, by *compromise,* we surrender parts of our souls in our attempts to satisfy other people, and we feel compelled to act or behave in ways that are contrary to our intuitive "gut feelings." This is in contrast to *accommodating* with temporary, voluntary behavior to comply with a silly rule or game. We can have fun playing "magic" with our three-year-olds with no loss of self-esteem. When we are self-assured and self-confident, we can voluntarily go along and cooperate in any social circumstances. This kind of conformity will even add to our self-images. The need for emotional maturity and for becoming independent individuals is never ending; however, for life's sake, we may, as infants, deprecate ourselves and compromise our individualities for the sake of approval from our families.

The emotional cost of attempting to be what others want us to be, rather then being ourselves, is horrendous. Pretense and tension result when we activate all our bodies' systems, especially our immune systems, in defensively play-acting, pretending to be persons other than the ones who are engraved in the templates in our genes. In defense, we turn our emotional energy back against ourselves by wanting the past to be different, or by embracing fears for the future. When we direct our emotional energy inward in a prolonged manner in ongoing preparatory actions, these emotional drains are destructive. This is the basic cause of most of today's ill health.

At the start, our dependency on our caretakers is complete, but we have diminishing needs throughout infancy and childhood. By adolescence, our physical dependency is completely ended, and by the age of thirty, we should have outgrown all vestiges of emotional dependency. The reality, in the adult world, is that we should not demand or expect acceptance from anyone but ourselves. As mature adults, our expectations of ourselves and others should be entirely in accord with attitudes of emotional maturity. But, is this generally the case?

Emotional dependence needs to be differentiated from adult cooperation and reliance. Dependence is characterized by feelings of incompleteness within ourselves and by the demand that others supply the lacking parts of us. In truly adult relationships, individuals voluntarily bond in a strong, reciprocal sense of esteem and caring. This arrangement affords each the added encouragement of the other by providing safe spaces in which both can develop more completely than either individual could separately.

As adults, we are separate entities, free of demanding that others emotionally accept us. When people elect to accept us, we may feel better, but for our own benefit, we accept the reality that we cannot earn, buy, or demand acceptance from other people, especially from family members. We are aware of our own limitations, in that we can accept others only to the degree that we accept ourselves. Acceptance is a very special life force. In a sense, it is like financial credit—when we have great financial assets and reserves, we can get unlimited credit almost anywhere. When we are secure in our self-acceptance, we will not beg, plead, or try to gain acceptance from others.

Acceptance cannot be earned. However, we can, by *doing*, earn approval and respect. Both approval and respect can be sustained only by continued performance. In contrast, acceptance is for *being*. To accept others is a very personal prerogative and the degree to which we can accept others is limited by how secure we feel within ourselves. *Respect* is the consolation prize we demand or strive for when we have already given up hope of having *esteem*, which can only come from being accepted as we are. The lowest level of regard is *respect,* which we demand or extort from others. It's the kind of regard we might extract with big guns or angry threats.

Our initial identities come from genetic encoding that is in every cell of our bodies and is present at birth. Innately, we feel that we are the only important persons, but our parents' acceptance or rejection of us may mandate modification of this attitude about ourselves. Our caretakers' acceptance of us is limited to the degree to which they accept themselves. We, by nature's design, take on their attitudes as we do their language, because our unconscious minds move toward whatever image is presented to them. If our caretakers' personal acceptance is only partial, we spend our lives begging or trying to have others accept us. This creates no-win situations, because the images that we have are fixed in our own subconscious minds, which depict those attitudes in which we picture ourselves as undesirable. If our parents assume that we are their personal belongings, then we feel that we are part of them, and we will have a difficult time establishing our separate identities.

To do things my way is great phrase, but in the long run, it represents merely the attitude of a two-year-old. Rather, to *be ourselves* is the appropriate drive for us as fulfilled human beings. It is an illusion to assume that we are in competition with others, or that we should model ourselves after our heroes or mentors. When we model ourselves after others, we have presupposed that *they* are more than we can be or will ever be. In pure activity, we can apply our potential to emulate the feats of others by *doing* the specialized skills they have perfected. However, our lives are too short to develop all of the potential talents that are encoded in our own specific genes. Life's goal is to fulfill our very special potentials to the degree that we can direct our emotional energies to those ends.

The degree to which we fulfill the potentials encoded in the templates of our genes will be determined by the degree to which we accept ourselves as we are. With full self-acceptance, we gain use of all of our emotional energies to experience the fullness of human development. Accompanying this acceptance, we will have our greatest number of options and maximum opportunities to participate and enjoy human interactions. Our achievement, or limited achievement, in emotional development will determine our quality of life.

The ultimate in self-esteem is to be totally accepting of ourselves. By virtue of our intuition, we are the only species that can be aware of the preordained potentials encoded in our personal genomes. Our feelings of well-being are in direct relationship to our sensing and actively fulfilling our potentials. We can accept others only to the extent that we accept ourselves. Because all of us come from a common ancestry, we can appreciate the common basic part of our human genome. That is, common behaviors that have allowed individuals to have separate identities have also mandated that humans band together in cooperative communities. Behavior that is in violation of the encoded supportive, generic human and individual templates will alert our intuitive senses and gut feelings that something is wrong. These signals are logically strongest at birth and can be reduced by emotional maladjustment but cannot be entirely eliminated.

The general principle is that when we are evolved, enlightened persons, we accept ourselves, for we have largely fulfilled the unique personal templates encoded in our genes. Our satisfaction with this life will be determined by the degree to which we sense that we are individuals, without compromising or adopting self-images demanded by anyone else.

Developing Attitudes

We were all infants once, and the first task we took on was to figure out what was going on around us. We did our best to make sense of the part of life we were experiencing and to try to see the rules by which things happened. In other words, we attempted to understand how life works and how we fit into it. In doing so, we naturally used the limited information available to us in our situation as dependent infants in our families. All humans face this task and we all draw some conclusions of enormous significance for our lives.

In the initial three years of life, we form our primary attitudes concerning our self-images, including how we regard ourselves and relate to others, and we form our self-esteem, self-worth, and self-assessments. Further, we establish ourselves in set positions within the pecking order among all other people. In the second three years, we form our attitudes concerning other people.

All live organisms, from one-celled animals to elephants with hundreds of trillions of cells, have inborn and developed defenses when threatened. At birth and in early infancy, our defense systems are rudimentary compared to those of adults. One type of defense we do use in infancy, especially early infancy, is blunting reception of those stimuli that are threatening to us, and as a consequence, we can become forever numbed to future responses.

Infants have no impressions of past threatening incidents; they have only the reactive-protective devices derived from gene-encoded instincts. When infants perceive threatening stimuli, they react defensively, similarly to primitive baby animals, and form withdrawal responses by numbing or blocking the reception of further such stimuli. Only after the age of two do imagery and fear, with specific conjoined defenses, begin to take shape and increasingly become the prominent protective mechanisms. After the age of three, this manner of acquisition of defenses supplants all reactively and protectively generated fears as described in *Full Share*.

During the first thirty-six months, children are in the process of developing billions of new synaptic connections, making it possible to analyze all the new information presented to them. Fear is a big issue; initially, in infancy, its development is in reaction to dangers identified solely by genetically recorded experiences—the reactive fears of ancient ancestors. In the first six months, infants lack the discretionary ability to analyze and evaluate all the information they receive. Infant brains respond instinctively to injurious stimuli without indexing them to personal previously recorded details and imagery, as they will do after the age of three. In later infancy and childhood, the acquisition of active fears requires a personal exposure to noxious stimuli, which initiates a subconscious recording of those specific incidences of alleged danger. The understanding of this mechanism was acquired in Ted's thirty-year practice of hypnoanalysis, during which he personally conducted thousands of age-reenactments.

Defenses become part of our belief systems and are apparent in our attitudes. There are two periods of defensive formation—infancy and young childhood. In the first, our initial thirty-six months, we are concerned only with ourselves, and we form our basic attitudes about our personal worth to guide us the rest of our lives. In the second period, ages three to six years, we assume our attitudinal adjustments in dealing with other people. All attitudes are age-related, that is, each develops at a specific age. Another way to understand age-related attitudes is to regard them as personality arrests.

Emotionally, personality arrests or age-related attitudes represent blocks and stabilizations of developmental growth in specific limited areas of our full individualities. In the initial formation, the intensity and the length of repeated exposure to emotional impact determines the intensity of the imprinting of these experiences in the formation of our various attitudes that will govern later behavior.

At birth, we exhibit behaviors that are directed by the rudimentary beliefs that are already installed in our brains by genetic encoding. Nature designed this encoding in order to get us safely through the birthing process and neonatal period. We come with the expectation that we will be accepted as we are. That is, we want to be accepted along with our dependency needs. In addition to being accepted, we want to be nurtured by our caretakers and aided in fulfilling our native drives in such areas as investigative curiosity, enthusiasm, and free emotional display. Only caretakers who communicate with us through intuition and attitude, touching and holding, can satisfy these powerful dependencies. When these needs are not fulfilled, but rather, are summarily rejected, we react by suspending further development and stabilizing our emotional growth at the corresponding points in our personality development. At these blocks in our emotional growth, we will develop protective bulkheads, personality arrests. Emotional arrests are created when there are no safe places for us in our environment, and therefore, we must create safe places within ourselves. On the other hand, if we are accepted as equal and separate individuals, we will continuously mature emotionally.

These early-formed protective bulkheads will be acted out as fears and expressed as attitudes of shame. This inward deprecation is evidence that we have had to stuff our natural, laudable feelings and replace them with contrite exhibitions of humility, by which behaviors we experience ourselves as being more acceptable to our parents. With shame, we do not like ourselves, because we perceive that we possess those particular traits that our caretakers do not like in us. We become ashamed of whom we are. Our adopted feelings never extinguish our basic needs for family members to accept us as the special individuals who are encoded in our DNA. However, reactive fears and crippling shame will semi-permanently, or forever, prevent us from letting down our guards and allowing ourselves to become emotionally close to them. Ironically, after nullifying our true identities in our fearfulness, out of necessity to survive, we become utterly emotionally dependent on our caretakers.

If we feel shameful about ourselves in any manner, then we feel undeserving, and in most of our lives' accomplishments, we act accordingly; we eventually fail or destroy ourselves. Witness the self destruction of Elvis Presley. All our lives, we can pretend to be the persons that our caretakers wanted us to be. Merely getting "atta-boys," or praise, does not elevate us or cancel the feelings of crippling shame about ourselves. Only revisions of early beliefs can upgrade our attitudes about our self-images. Consequently, just changing our perceptions of our self-worth will have an enduring effect on our basic attitudes and their direction of our behavior.

Attitude is Age Related

Our modern computers have default settings that automatically control the procedures of every program, unless we consciously strive to change them. Our bodies have comparably programmed default attitude systems to automatically regulate behavior, unless we make conscious efforts to abridge them. All beliefs are from the past, and they were formed at precise moments. The data from which this system is derived and assembled comes solely from the information that is available to our minds at those specific times of our lives. The composition and complexity of beliefs at any given time is determined by our brains' neural development acquired up to those stages of our lives, and by the extent of our mental abilities at those times.

In the first six years of life, this program is fashioned by day to day and minute to minute experiences. Our beliefs then function unconsciously to determine our perceptions and reactions, just like computer software functions unseen to determine what the computer will do with data.

After the age of six, our enlarging attitudes are essentially composed of compounds of the attitudes that we feel obliged to assume for protection of our individualities during our first half dozen years of life.

Emotional reactions are attitudes from fixed beliefs that are tied directly to the times at which we adopted them. Our defenses are the fixed products of those stages of sophistication of our nervous systems at the times of their adoption.

There are two distinct divisions to the types of attitudes that we all have. The first type is established in infancy (birth to the age of three) and is entirely infantile. The second (ages three through six) is protective and childish.

Intuitively, as infants, we are primarily dedicated to staying alive, and our secondary essential thrust is to establish our own *personal identities*. Initially, we are concerned only about ourselves, with zero ability to be concerned or considerate of others. Characteristically, only toward the end of our third year do we naturally begin to become aware of and concerned about our effect on others.

In general, these emotional attitudes are self protective and defensive. That defense is present to guard us from our greatest threat, that of other people intruding upon our personal identities.

The period of childhood, ages three to six, is the normal time for the development of socialization in children. In general, during this childhood period, our developing attitudes are still for our own benefit and protection. With our increasing awareness of others, our attitudes are focused on our interactions with other people, that is, how we regard them, and how they respond to us.

The nature of our beliefs and defenses changes with age. Those developing in infancy are mainly concerned with ourselves, while those developing in childhood are mainly concerned with others. The next section focuses on development in infancy.

Emotional Development as Reflected in Attitude

Let us review the usual behaviors at the stages of development in the first three years:

Newborn:

We are totally obsessed with staying alive and alleviating discomfort. Anger (turning into rage) is the prime method of getting attention and respect and declaring our separate individualities. At this stage, we are absolutely unconcerned about Mother's, or anyone else's, discomfort or inconvenience. We are totally impatient and demanding.

First weeks:

Early social development, the heart of which is learning to trust, begins. We rely on intuition and reading of caretakers' attitudes as they respond to our needs. We establish routines.

One month:

We begin to have awareness of people, especially through touch. We thrust our arms and legs, learn to expect help, and learn whether connectedness to others is available or not.

One to three months:

We become quiet and calm when held and snuggled and learn to turn on the charm. We repeat our parents' responses. Predictability begins to build trust, and we love consistency.

3 months:

Our trust in our caretakers builds every time they help us. We learn patterns of behavior. Repetition of prompt responses to our needs builds trust, and predictability creates security.

4 to 6 months:

Everything is a game. We drop things on the floor that our caretakers will pick up. We cover and uncover our faces. We may become interested in strangers. We become highly imitative of actions, moods, and behaviors. We take pleasure in accomplishments. We learn every day from watching those around us.

5 months:

We express anger when others take away things that we want. We increasingly seek approval by watching our parents. Now, our confidence is reinforced or undermined.

1 to 6 months:

We demand food

.

6 to 12 months:

We especially need support in our attempts to explore. Overprotective or anxious parents may limit our curiosity and exploration. We may seek parental assistance with everything. Repetition is the key to learning. We enjoy routine.

13 to 14 months:

Negativism begins and reasoning does not work. We begin to form our beliefs as to whether or not we are responsible for others' feelings.

15 to 18 months:

Negativism and independence are expressed as defiance—"No." We continuously want approval for what we do, which in reality means we want *acceptance of who we are.* If we are emotionally arrested when we are very immature, we cannot distinguish disapproval of our actions from rejection of our separate and distinct individualities. We now study how objects differ from each other and how they are alike. It is easier to learn good behavior and self-control now than at any other time in our lives. Imitation is the driving force. We may enjoy performing routines of our own creation for others; we like applause. We need to win occasionally and have our own way. Bumbling, impulsiveness, and thrusting dominate here as our motor skills develop. We need protection from our own impulsiveness. Our lack of abilities upsets us. At this age, we do not like our personal spaces invaded by strangers.

16 to 24 months:

We may go off by ourselves when emotionally confused or upset.

21 months:

We are self-centered. Almost all take and no give is our rule here. We have very little desire or need to please.

2 years:

In stores, we walk off with anything within reach. We express possession: "My mommy, my daddy." We play in parallel. We say, "Mine," and snatch and grab. We can express warm emotions. We explore with touch, taste, and smell. We get into everything. We strew and smear. Routines suit us again.

2 ½ years:

We take the opposite direction our parents have chosen. We demand sameness, but like to explore and investigate. We set up rituals for ourselves and others, and thereby avoid the conflict of making choices. We vacillate back and forth, as in the choice of chocolate or vanilla. We may be imperious, bossy, and demanding, not because we are sure, but because we are unsure. We are almost totally unable to modulate, and we are made up of extremes. We insist that, "Mommy do it." Things are more important than people are. We are self-centered. We strike over property rights. "Me," "Mine," "I need," are often said. We find it extremely difficult to take turns. Seldom are we able to resolve our own altercations without adult supervision. We want specific objects.

2 to 3 years:

Now we may begin to recognize which behaviors are approved and which are not.

As emotionally mature adults, we may choose to use some or all of these behaviors, but our underlying attitudes are mature, not infantile or childish. The difference here is voluntary choice. The two can be readily differentiated by using our intuition or by testing. If we feel *compelled* to automatically defend any behaviors, there are problems. When we feel compelled to automatically *defend* our attitudes, we have problems in our emotional maturity, that is, emotional hang-ups. Entirely different emotional emanations come from us when we're threatened, and when we're merely stating the position of our attitudes.

Ultimate Emotional Development

Horticulturists growing orange trees manage their orchards to grow the best trees, which produce premium fruit. They know, by observation, the characteristics of the ultimate orange tree. Similarly, specifications for the ultimately physically evolved human being are common knowledge. Informed parents have this image in mind as they support and nourish their children to maximize their physical development. Logically, caretakers of infants should also be mindful of ultimate emotional development and be active in aiding and assisting normal emotional growth patterns, while protecting their infants from harmful deterrents. Care is needed, especially in the first three years, when infants desperately require encouragement and support for their emerging natural emotional characteristics. In addition to protecting their infants, parents should shelter them from caretakers whose aims are to actively train the infants, because such early training will result in the infants taking on the prejudicial social attitudes of their trainers and making performing to please others more important than being their own persons. This forced artificial molding can only be done at the expense of compromising the children's own normal self-identities.

The characteristics of ultimately emotionally evolved humans include two essential elements: self-acceptance and openness.

Foremost, as ultimately emotionally evolved humans, we accept ourselves for being our own persons, that is, for being distinct individuals as we fulfill the potentials of our own DNA. In normal emotional evolution, the seeking of acceptance from others will be discontinued at puberty. Increasing self-acceptance can only be achieved when we, as teenagers, have strong self-identities, which should be accomplished in our first thirty-six months. *Being our own persons* is entirely apart from begging for approval from others for *doing our own things.* "Doing things my way" is an outstanding characteristic of two-year-olds.

As evolved individuals, we are warm, open, and loving. We will not model ourselves after other people or heroic images. Our whole thrust and goal is to seek fulfillment of the potentials that we have in the templates encoded in our genes. Self-acceptance is the pinnacle of emotional maturity. From this vantage point, we can devote all our emotional energy to the present. We withdraw all of the energy that we may have formerly invested in the past, when we wanted the world to be different. In addition, we stop investing energy in fear for the future. When we direct our minds emotionally to live only in the present, then we are in the state of enlightenment.

Our observations and findings over the past fifty years are that the overriding cause of emotional distress, and of at least one-half of all medical illness, is the adoption of infantile or childish attitudes that block normal emotional development. Our adopted attitudes from tribal customs, family prejudices, and other people prevent us from being our own persons. The adoption and the reenactment of behaviors that reflect age related attitudes are the cardinal causes of dysfunctional society. That is, any time we are driven by attitudes that cause us to behave in infantile or childish manners, harmonious interpersonal relationships are disrupted.

As parents, our job is to protect our children from conditioning circumstances that will force developing individuals to form, from parental pressures and environment, self protective attitudes. Our children's personal emotional integrities are composed of all instances in which they are forced to form self protections, that is, required to take upon themselves someone else's programs or attitudes, rather than following their own agendas encoded in their genes. Attitudes coupled with often unrealistic expectations then govern behavior throughout our entire lives.

We, as individuals, for our prospective development, have a two-part theme to our specific gene patterns. The primary theme is to become human animals distinct from all other mammals; the secondary theme is to enable ourselves to develop our unique potentials to become distinct among all other humans. Our blueprints afford us tremendous possibilities, but limit us in our ultimate attainment in some categories. That is, we may be especially gifted in art or mathematics, but limited in musical pitch. Especially unique to normal humans is the faculty for oral and written language. Also, man has the special ability for developing social behavior that is uniquely human. When we are allowed to evolve normally, following our specific genetic templates, we will have the special characteristic of self-acceptance and the capacity to accept others as they are.

As normal two-year-olds, we can be expected to explore endlessly as we make up our minds definitely every few minutes. When we are constantly thwarted in new explorations, we learn to be cautious and that we are not safe to just do it. To protect ourselves, we form attitudes of indecisiveness by doing nothing spontaneously, preventing criticism and probable punishment. Throughout later life, this learned life saving maneuver, which feels like it has worked dependably for years, cannot be wantonly discontinued. The attitude of indecisiveness is a protective bulkhead. Many other examples of protective bulkheads will be depicted throughout this book.

Language, dialect, and the basic rules of human interaction are taught to us, as infants, almost wholly by example. If a three-month-old infant is trapped in his crib while his parents are arguing with life threatening intensity, he will witness a forceful demonstration that they lack esteem for one another as well as esteem for themselves. With repeated exposure, he will adopt an attitude of no esteem for himself. Later, this attitude of feeling totally undeserving may enable that infant to become a prostitute or bag lady or career homeless person.

Experience teaches that there is only one reason for doing anything, which is, *we want to.* When Mother repeatedly asks, "Why?" we, as four-year-olds, must respond. We have been doing what we wanted to do, but Mother will not accept this answer. She demands, under the threat of rejection or death that we tell her what she wants to hear, so we make up fictitious answers to assuage her impending anger. We cultivate this protective device of lying, which becomes a semi-permanent attitude about truthfulness to serve us the rest of our lives. We have had a government official in a high office who behaves with the attitude of a four-year-old. He acts as if his life depends on his giving any acceptable answer to his voters. Incidentally, if we see no problem with his answers, then we share the same four-year-old attitudinal dysfunction that he has.

When we are utterly dependent and are

confronted by life-threatening situations, we are forced to take on other people's attitudes simply to survive. This would be a normal reaction for us at twelve months of age, when we have no ability to critically examine or search for reasons. The necessity for assuming our parents' attitudes causes our self-images and self-esteem to be compromised. Further, if we continue to defend these attitudes, then in this regard, our self-esteem will not improve for the rest of our lives. The more we are compromised for *being,* the less we trust ourselves or others. We are less attractive because we are less genuine. This does not mean we cannot find places in our society; it only means that we will settle for approval for what we can do for others rather than acceptance for *who we are.*

Notice that there are two parts to the process of forming our life's attitudes: What our parents did, and what we concluded about ourselves based on what they did. Our parents did whatever they did; their behavior became formative for us only when we decided it meant something specific about us and how the world works. From that moment on, we lived out the result of that belief, to our benefit or harm. Thus, we are not actually victims of our parents' behavior, but of our own beliefs.

The good news is that we have always been in the driver's seat and still are today. The problems and limitations of our lives are the result of our continuing to live out the beliefs we first formed without re-examining them, or even remembering where, when, or why we formed them. Upgrading those beliefs to serve us better is the path to ultimate emotional development and will affect every part of our lives.

Correlation of Fear and Defense

If we are afforded continuous acceptance for being separate and equal individuals throughout our emotionally formative years, our natural paths will result in our becoming adults who are warm, open, and accepting.

As infants, our very survival depends on whether we are accepted or rejected by our parents. When our natural emotional evolutionary paths are blocked by threats of death or rejection, then, for the sake of our individualities, we must develop protective mechanisms. In order to continue more limited emotional survival beyond interruption points, we automatically generate defenses designed to avoid and counteract any vaguely similar threats that may occur in the near or distant future. Obligatory defenses become part of our beliefs, our attitudes, and our personalities. In times of stress, if they are not revised or removed, these defenses will forever control and limit our basic behavior to the lowest common denominator.

When other people recognize or challenge any aspect of our arrested personal identities, our attitudes become apprehensive, suspicious, or fearful. Also, in an instant, others can be alerted, because we display attitudes of preparedness and of being on-guard, which represent our insecurities. For all fears, our subconscious minds retain active images of the initial threatening incidents. These images are inseparably joined with detailed defense templates of action. All specific fears, coupled with their special defense programs, will be in readiness, because they remain in our subconscious minds, continuously draining energy. These complexes become a part of our basic beliefs and our self-images.

We have unlimited capacities to accumulate fears, coupled with their defenses, designed for instant actions to cope with all contingencies in the future that are vaguely reminiscent of our past bad experiences. The maintenance of ready defense plans adds to an accumulating energy drain. We have limited daily emotional energy. That energy which is dedicated to defense will have priority over all the emotional energy for the present—energy we might otherwise use for discretion or enjoyment. This is the price of our security, because these mandatory defenses make us feel protected in our isolated, private, safe places. The more defenses we maintain, the smaller and more restricted will be our lives.

The next priority of energy entitlement is that which is required to contend with the daily upkeep of living, and finally, we have that residual emotional energy that we may use for purely elective activities and interpersonal relationships.

Anger from the past and all emotional investitures in wanting the past to be different, and also fear of the future, take priority, keeping our bodies on ready alert. They are constant emotional drains on our time and energy. They rob from us the discretionary portions of our energy that we might use to live in the present. They decrease our choices to have quality of life now. *The present is the only real time that we have* to interact with our families and friends. When we can eliminate both collections of emotional charges, that is, wanting the past to be different and fear of the future, then we can have all our energy available for the present. To come to terms with the past, we need to release former emotions and convert untoward incidents into merely historical memories. Additionally, we need to replace all fear with preparedness programs, by gathering adequate information of the relative dangers. More simply, we convert fear into understanding of specific dangers. Then we are in the state of enlightenment, free of untoward emotion relating to the past or the future. Only then can we truly be fully present with the persons in whose company we may be.

With emotional maturity and the understanding of real and specific dangers, we can replace fears with attendant defense plans. A thorough knowledge of situations and the release of emotions convert fear into understanding, in that we are aware of dangerous potentials, and awareness of those dangers no longer arouses emotions. With awareness and respect, we can devise defense plans, like fire drills. Factual disaster plans require no emotional energy to sustain them, because they are merely factual.

Protective emotional bulkheads are similar to bulkheads on naval vessels. When ships are under attack, watertight doors are secured to prevent adjacent compartments from being flooded. By nature's design, when we are under attack, we can form emotional bulkheads, which are designed for temporary protection. They provide safe compartments, in which we can sustain, intact, all of our previously attained emotional growth with its streams of belief, which are parts of our identities. Logically, the bulkheads should be opened when the current danger has passed. However, if the initiating incidents have enough emotional trauma attending them, the bulkheads become more permanent. These bulkheads temporarily, often permanently, prevent further growth in the involved emotional streams.

From the moment emotional defenses are adopted, similar threats will provoke instant automatic life saving responses, generated and governed by the midbrain. To appreciate the speed of this response, we need to compare it to our ability to grab a coin in midair that just slipped out of our hands. No cognitive thought is required. If the stimulus to activate our voluntary action had to be routed through a whole series of neurons up to the highest brain centers of conscious thought and returned back through still another set of neurons, this delayed action would make us too late to catch the coin mid air. In general, this is the way we are put together—we act first and think later. Also, it is natural for us to rationalize, explain, and justify our actions after the fact.

Purely mechanical reactions and the execution of learned and practiced living habits require no thoughtful deliberation. Moreover, such reactions, which sustain our attitudes and our identities, will trigger our defenses in microseconds. The most telltale evidence of emotional immaturity is demonstrated when we "go off half cocked" in protestation, argumentation, and anger. The whole truth is that, *whenever we become emotionally defensive, it is because we feel vulnerable and exposed due to some emotional immaturities that demand automatic defenses.*

When we are free of stress and pressure, we can act out adult type behaviors in presenting our self-portraits. However, in time of stress, when we are incapacitated due to illness, or when we are experiencing the influence of drugs or alcohol, we lose our ability to act out our standard charades. Our behavior is no longer voluntary, but rather automatically infantile and/or childish, and reactive. The reaction reverts back to our infantile or childish feelings of safety under the protective bulkheads that we established early in our emotional development. The degree to which we revert to those protective areas varies with the emotional pressure we feel. The traits of infantile or childish behavior are age-related, and in turn are pegged to our beliefs about our integrities and our estimates of ourselves in relation to the human pecking order and how we must relate to our fellow men. Our behavior will vary relative to the various attitudes about the many aspects of our self-worth, including our evaluations of ourselves and others as to acceptance, confidence, right to exist, trustworthiness, capability, and esteem. We can use our conscious minds without stress to control our voluntary muscles, as long as those actions do not attempt to override our basic defense systems, which are mediated by our self-images and belief systems in our subconscious minds.

As much as we might want to consider ourselves to be self regulated, independent, mindful persons, in control of our own ideations and wills, we are only about five percent correct. The reality is that our nervous systems are designed to relieve us of the tedium of rethinking and relearning repetitive actions and habits and recreating defenses. We have used these semiautomatic devices once before or thousands of times already, because they have repeatedly saved our lives by enabling our defensive reactions to past alleged threats.

These repetitive housekeeping functions are mediated in the midbrain, which is located at the top of the spinal cord beneath the cerebral cortex. From this area, our subconscious minds manage our autonomic nervous systems. Our sympathetic and parasympathetic nervous systems have the function to direct and coordinate the tension of our muscles, regulate our cardiovascular systems, modulate secretions of our glands, control gastrointestinal, genital, and urinary functions, as well as to execute our habit patterns, dominate our defense reactions, and most of all, maintain all of our fixed beliefs and attitudes.

When we pit the cognitive parts of our conscious minds, mainly located in our cerebral cortexes, against the subconscious parts of our minds, mainly situated in our midbrain regions, the subconscious prevails. When we recognize that 95% of our bodies are directed by our subconscious minds, we understand that 95% of all our actions and behaviors are automatically initiated.

Accordingly, the great bulk of any therapy involving behaviors, beliefs, and attitudes should be dedicated to learning how to direct our subconscious minds. All our lives, we have formed habit patterns and life saving defenses, which are all housed in and coordinated by our subconscious minds in our midbrains. Although our conscious minds control our decision making and cognitive thinking, they control only about 5% of our bodies' machinery—mainly the voluntary muscles.

The more we practice defenses, habits, or skills, the more they become entrenched. Our prejudices and fears are also strengthened with practice and repetition. Likewise, the more we use our protective emotional bulkheads, the more readily they are activated. When habits or defenses are only infrequently practiced or lightly entrenched, we can, consciously and temporarily, willfully override these responses. With frequent and persistent overriding, we may form revised habits or defenses. However, when we are harried, or under great stress, the continuing practice of supplanting habits or defenses requires more emotional energy than we have available, because our conscious minds are overloaded, and we will revert back to our old behaviors.

Remember, our conscious minds have only a few clear channels on which to operate, while our subconscious minds have thousands of coordinated pathways to control organ function, muscle tone, and emotions.

As part of the formation of our beliefs, fears initiate the formation of defense or avoidance templates, which constitute personality arrests and are incorporated into our self-images—what we most deeply believe ourselves to be—and our self-worth. There are fewer personality arrests formed in infancy, ages birth to three, than in childhood, ages three to six. However, the attitudes of infancy are much harder to deal with and are more resistant to revision, and their effect is also more general and distressing.

In our society, there is a great premium and reward to being in control. The emotional effort and energy that we expend to pretend to be constantly in control and socially correct is directly proportional to the number and intensity of the personality arrests that we have formed in infancy and early childhood. We experience tremendous stress pretending to be grown-up and socially or politically correct, or even acceptable, in adult society. The more we attempt this, the more often, and to a greater degree, will we tend to revert to acting out the infants or children within us. All of us are emotionally impaired to some degree. Universally, the *stress of pretense,* small or great, creates the longing to relax, get high, drunk, or stoned.

Quite simply, the harder we have to pretend to be grown-up by acting out to conform to our self-portraits, the more stress we are under. When we have multiple arrests in our emotional growth, accrued early and imbedded with highly emotional fright, these fixations become most resistant to revision or even to the temporary pretense that they do not exist. These underlying attitudes, reflecting infantile or childish beliefs about the world and its dangers, sabotage our attempts in fantasy to idealize ourselves and enact our self-portraits. Society requires us to be grown-up and to control ourselves, and under peaceful circumstances, we want to fit in or conform to a certain degree. This is possible only if we are emotionally mature and there is practically no stress. In fact, when we are mature, we will be stressed when we feel some need to adjust to groups of immature people, either children or adults, for whom we feel we should temporarily make a voluntary adjustment by interacting at their infantile or childish levels.

Pretending to be adults, when our self-images are those of dependent infants or needy children, can cause us terrific, sustained stress. Some of this is lessened when we find, and align ourselves with, groups or gangs who generally behave in our own childish or infantile manners. A most favored way of reducing stress is to join groups that expect less of us and possibly use alcohol or drugs that so impair us that we expect less of ourselves, and thereby, fit in. This is best illustrated in those who join escalating, raging mobs. Conversely, if we recognize the development of mob mentality, and there is nothing we can do to quell the turmoil, then, as emotionally mature persons, we will distance ourselves from the scene.

When we have only a few clusters of personality arrests in childhood, ages three to six, alcohol works well to relax the pretense of having everything under control, because our stress is relieved by the impairment of drinking. If we continue to imbibe, we will get slurred in speech and uncoordinated in muscle action outwardly, but our basic personalities do not change.

In our experience working with hundreds of alcoholics, we have observed that, when under the influence, they behave with personalities that would be expected in normal children at the age of two-and-a-half years. At this level of maturity, individuals are interested only in themselves. Almost all of these people also express and exhibit *feelings of unworthiness*, the hallmark of alcoholism. The influence of ethanol causes them to behave like two-and-a-half-year-old children who are out of control. Pharmacologically, ethyl alcohol is a suppressant. As the addicted persons consume larger and larger doses of ethanol, they progressively inhibit all adult-like behaviors and retrograde, until they reach the state of obnoxious two-and-a-half-year-olds who are "doing their own things." They are finally free of social refinements and restraints. Their perceptions can well be that they are having a high old time, because all their pretenses of decorum are temporarily gone. Characteristically, they seek out other two-and-a-half-year-olds so they can revel together.

Our experience with hard drug addicts, such as cocaine and heroine users, is that, in addition to many of the same dysfunctions that afflict a good portion of our society, they have personality arrests of infancy. Their belief systems almost universally include *feelings of shame and worthlessness*. Their behavior poignantly demonstrates this attitude; when they are totally under the influence, they place zero value on their families, friends, rules, and the law. Their only objective is to do what furthers their selfish ends and is immediately gratifying. This is classic infantile behavior. The use of hard drugs can cause temporary complete release from responsibility and the pretense of being grown up, but when the buzz wears off, users again experience those terrible feelings of shame and worthlessness. When they are clean and sober, they face the immense stress of pretending to be much more emotionally mature than they feel themselves to be.

When it comes to emotional maturity, we have a heterogeneous mix in society. Those in similar states of emotional evolution tend to group together. This is somewhat like people of like incomes finding greater acceptance with those who can afford a life style similar to their own. Alcohol and addictive drugs can serve to bring individuals down to their base levels of emotional growth. If individuals take part in successful remedial emotional therapy, and they succeed in obtaining more emotional maturation, they usually find that they have fewer interests in common with their old friends.

Affirmation of an Infant

One of most gratifying aspects of rearing babies from birth is observing their day by day changes in physical growth, mechanical aptitude, and especially, evolving emotional development. Most fascinating is their wonderment about new objects and especially, their personal delight as they learn new maneuvers and acquire added physical dexterity.

Our job as parents during the three years of infancy is to provide safe places for our children, so that they will feel good about themselves and develop strong self identities. Their DNA predetermines not only their physical and intellectual potentials, but more importantly, their individual, human, emotional identities, that is, their predetermined individualism. The guiding rule is to regard and treat children as separate and equal. If this attitude about their self-images is not accomplished during infancy, it is extremely difficult to create after the age of three. Children do not need to be praised or patted on the head like a pet dog who has just fetched a stick, but they do need to know that what they just did is OK, and that they are going in a good direction. At this tender age of learning, it is important that they please themselves, not us. We make it safe when they are ready to progress, and we encourage them to keep going and doing whatever they have initiated. It is reasonable and desirable to acknowledge to our babies that, in their activities, they are pleasing us, but it is essential that they be rewarded with our acceptance of who they are.

Consider the distinction between happiness and fulfillment. Happiness is ethereal and is soon forgotten. We feel fulfillment when we reach new levels of accomplishment and development or reveal talents. With each step of our children's developing potentials, their self-images are larger and their self-esteem more secure. These are permanent attainments and cannot be taken from them. Praising our children may make them temporarily happy. But if they are purposefully acting just to please us, then they put themselves in the position in which we may require them to keep repeating these acts to constantly receive "atta- boys" by performing stunts that they really do not care to do. If, however, for their own sakes, they gain new skills or further develop talents, they will sense inward feelings of satisfaction, whether or not their parents acknowledge them. Our children do not need praise for doing, but rather, to establish self-esteem, they need sincere acceptance and support in their own senses of fulfillment.

Babies, by their nature, are self-centered and demand that their needs and wants be cared for. They are totally occupied with pleasing themselves; this is their normal and genetically prescribed attitude. They are in this world not to please or love us, but for their own survival and development. To ensure normal emotional evolution, the younger they are, the less we should require any type of behavior or performance of them. We need to provide them with safe places and encourage them to be their own persons and to experientially do their own things. We acknowledge and encourage their own individual flow as they sample their environment. We may safely trust that they will learn everything we could teach them simply by watching us and imitating everything we do without instruction.

When, for our own amusement, we require them to do specific actions or perform any tricks as demonstrations for others, we usurp and frustrate their initiative. Such commands as, "Give mother a kiss," and "Wave bye-bye," can and should be delayed until, by prolonged demonstration, our babies can and will voluntarily imitate us. It will take months and years of increasing development before our babies' nervous systems and brains have all of their neurons. To expect and demand performances from them before they are neurologically capable will impair, delay, or possibly prevent their normal emotional evolution. We have all been taught not to trust babies to develop fully through their own innate initiative, but they are capable of doing so.

Goals

Goal setting and attainment are characteristic human behaviors. When we reach goals, we may lose our senses of direction, as in reaching the North Pole. However, when we choose directions with no end in sight, we enjoy the travel, for every day we accomplish our objectives. When our interests are broad and our drives strong, we create many new options during our challenging journeys. The essence of youthful life is having many choices, and we are constantly discovering those many alternate pathways on which to travel in our chosen directions. When we remain open to choices, we will come upon new opportunities that we could not possibly have seen before we started out on life's journey. To have unlimited choices requires that we have strong self-images, for without the reassurance of self-acceptance, weak self-images become increasingly encumbered with prohibiting fears that blind us to intriguing, alternate routes.

When we want the world to be different or better, while at the same time, we resist any changes or growth in ourselves, we are out of reality. Whenever, by force, we attempt to change or dominate ourselves or others, we prevent the development and fulfillment of our, and their, normal potentials, which are part of the templates encoded in the DNA. All personal emotional growth can come only when we upgrade our belief systems, and our expectations become realistic.

The primary good we can do for others is to provide them with safe places in which they have opportunities for self-energized growth. In personal development, we are the only ones who can sufficiently manage our minds to release ourselves from stifling old beliefs. By nature's design, we cannot forcefully change ourselves. When we forcefully attempt to change ourselves, we automatically resist. Only when we are open to the reception of added valid information, will we allow ourselves to make upward attitude adjustments for the resumption of our own normal emotional growth. If we count all the people who, since our birth, have attempted to force us, "for our own good," into molds that they considered essential for our becoming the "right kind of persons," we see that the more we are pressured, the more we must resist. Further, of all of those who pressured us, who has been the most persistent? We will find that *we are the ones* who, above all others, have been the most demanding of ourselves. Therefore, by the laws of nature, we will resent and sabotage ourselves most quickly in all attempts to forcefully command change in ourselves. Universally, the eventual result of continuously pressuring others to change will be that they will learn to avoid us, or, in the case of small children, they will learn to shut us out and not hear us.

Of all the criticizing people on our backs, we are the most persistent all our lives. Because we cannot avoid ourselves, we create our own internal turmoil when we attempt to force ourselves to be different. Only when we allow reception of added information about ourselves will our attitudes change. The reception of additional valid information will automatically revise former beliefs, which, in turn, will upgrade our attitudes, self-images, and emotional development. When our attitudes change, we automatically behave differently. This is the only viable path to creating unlimited options on our chosen paths in life.

Intuition

In spite of our declarations that we want to be special and unique, our behavior will disclose that, throughout our lives, we have worked at being the same as everyone else. Or, at least we've made efforts to be liked or have things that, among our peers, are considered to be in good taste, proper, or in style. Throughout the world, there is a great variety of languages, customs, and life styles, but these differences are getting smaller. In our electronic age, there is a great homogenizing process, so the world and culture is taking on sameness while we all protest that we want to be considered unique.

When we analyze our quality of life, we will find that is largely dependent on how well we get along with other people and the degree of mutual acceptance we experience. Therefore, we should focus on the very basis of this acceptance. It is obvious that understanding of languages, customs, and mores is helpful, but there is a whole realm of sameness that is far more important, namely, the human genome. Although greatly underused, we have a tremendously rich inheritance encoded in our genes, which can only be approached through the use of intuition, or in other words, gut feelings.

The premise that every human on the face of this earth is a descendant of a common African mother, who lived some millions of years ago, is entirely acceptable to us. Certainly, there is wide variation in a very limited number of distinct genes in our chromosomes, yet these chromosomes themselves are the same in every person on earth. For comparison, consider the Monarch butterfly in regard to the enormous amount of information that is encoded in the genes of every cell of this insect. The Monarch butterflies of eastern North America create four or five new generations each summer. The last generation, the fall generation, migrates thousands of miles to spend the winter in the rare Oyamel fir forests in the Michoacán highlands south of the Tropic of Cancer. In the spring, the butterflies mate and fly northward, laying eggs along the way, until a generation reaches the original North American home, and the process repeats. Each of the butterflies' cells' templates contains information about the world and the necessary instructions in navigation and propagation. This vast library of information is, in essence, the common bond which relates one Monarch butterfly to every other Monarch butterfly.

Consider that mankind has traveled much farther along the evolutionary path than the butterfly, and that we are the direct descendants of our ancestors. As we continue to develop the unique neocortex of the brain, we tend to increasingly attempt, by study and practice, to emphasize and elevate logic as being the epitome of human development. A large segment of today's society believes that people who are able to think and behave logically possess the finest quality of being human. When we put tremendous emphasis on being logical, we do this at the expense of assigning less and less credence to the ability to be intuitive, which is actually the best of our inheritance. Our intellectual striving works just fine in building bridges and developing computers, but is over emphasized at the expense of submerging our intuition, almost to the point of extinction.

Intuition is our sixth sense. Our first five senses—sight, sound, touch, taste, and smell—keep us in touch with our physical surroundings. Our sixth sense, intuition, keeps us in touch with ourselves. The most easily recognized facet of intuition is an inward awareness when we are required to behave contrarily to the encoding that is inscribed in our generic and individual DNA. This awareness is best recognized as our gut feelings of discomfort with any actions or proposed actions that are not in accord with the successful survival behavior that is inscribed in our genetic blueprints.

If we have developed emotionally to at least the age of three, we have consciences. Our troubled consciences are related to the feeling that the actions that we have taken, or are about to take, are out of accord with our rules of behavior, which we adopted and/or which were forcefully imposed upon us, usually by our parents. The feeling of conscience is the consequence of failing, or contemplating transgression of, these acquired rules of behavior. In its true sense, this is sin.

Intuition, on the other hand, is distinct from conscience. Our intuition is best recognized as our gut awareness, and can come from any cell in our bodies, although it is generally felt in the abdomen. This feeling, or sense, lets us know if the actions we have taken, or are about to take, are in accord with the successful survival behaviors that are inscribed in our genetic blueprints, both generic and individual.

All of us come into this world with forty-six generic chromosomes, with similarly encoded genes dedicated to human survival techniques. These include a total collection of the history of successful interactions of all our ancestors. To understand and relate to others, we need to search inwardly to regain and reinforce our intuition. Primarily through this mutual concordance of imagery, we can, by the use of interactive intuition, cement successful relationships. This is the basis for all profound interpersonal feelings. Native   Americans believe that we should become one with nature. That is a great goal, especially when we, as hunter-gatherers, are immediately dependent on the earth to sustain us. However, in modern life, we need to become one with all other human beings. We can do this only by understanding our commonality with all other people.

The deep understanding of universal human genetic inheritance can only be recognized through our intuition.

Ideally, when we are small infants, operating entirely on genetic instructions, our parents should do everything possible to bring to awareness and strengthen our belief in our own intuition, which, in reality, is ourselves. This is the link to our ancestral past, because we have the same format for emotional operational equipment that is present in all other human beings.

We voluntarily present ourselves to the world with our personas. How closely these portrait enactments coincide with the individual blueprints in our genetic encoding will define our comfort levels and feelings of security in society. In times of relatively low stress, we can act out the portraits of the characters we would like ourselves to be—this is normal and expected. The serious problem is brought about when, as infants, for our lives' sake, we are constantly obliged to play character portraits of children whose emotional behavior is only what our caretakers find acceptable.

Each time our defense systems force us to behave according to our caretakers' distorted models, our intuition will cause us to have uncomfortable gut feelings. This is the signal that our behaviors and pretenses are at variance with the encoded genetic blueprints that are very special to us personally, and, consequently, our feelings of self-esteem are compromised. We have sold our souls. There is only one element in self-esteem—trusting our intuition.

We can learn and practice investing our emotional energy into our gut feelings, the feelings that are present before we think. Intuition is the use of a primitive conception of the world and circumstance; it involves no deliberation or comparison, except what we previously learned throughout the generations of experience of our predecessors. The very act of searching by active thinking suppresses intuition, as if it were timid wild animals frightened by searchlights. We can be still and sense spontaneous thoughts, trusting our innermost revelations. All conjectural thought involves millions of neurons, but genetic insight and perception require no active thought, but is recorded in each cell of our bodies.

To understand our intuition, we must cease defending or justifying any of our ideas. When we share ideas and beliefs, we expand our insight. We should always be ready to describe our new inspirations in detail. However, *no thought needs defending.* Defending is an entirely different process, which, by its own nature, creates no new thought. Before we adopt or act on new ideas, we need to gauge them by our gut feelings. When we consider ideas relating to human interaction, we find there are probably no new thoughts or ideas, for they have all been considered before. We can notice what happens in this book, and the first book, *Full Share*, when principles are set forth for consideration. Does each principle feel right? If it does not resonate with what is already in our bodies, then we should ignore it. It is simply presented for consideration and is valuable only to the extent to which it is recognized as inherently true.

All explanations are generated in the neocortex, mostly in the left brain, which, for right handed people, is the dominant hemisphere. Zealous use of the left brain can block most creative ideas from the right brain. Alternatively, when we eventually have collections of images and ideas in our right brains, then we can use our left brains to evaluate and assess the relative worth and feasibility of one image over the others.

We can see or feel the images of what we want to accomplish, and then use these as a direction only. A tightly inscribed goal will severely restrict any additional ideas and images that will pop into our heads. Thinking that is rigid and fixed is like that of a fearful three-year-old who can, for his life's sake, defend only a single idea.

Again, we would like to emphasize the concept of *fulfillment* as opposed to *happiness*. Happiness has the element of satisfaction by attainment. We're happy when we get things we want. These acquisitions can be ethereal. Fulfillment, on the other hand, comes when we have developed some of our natural talents. Fulfillment cannot be taken away, nor can we ever return to our lesser selves.

We who have survived to this day did so by following most of the intuitional guidance derived from experiences of all those before us. Primarily, this information included the know-how to survive in nature and also in social interactions with one another. These principles are the gut feelings that allow mothers to be driven to care for their infants, and also dictate right and wrong in dealing with others.

In recapitulation of animal development, we as humans, started as single-celled animals. When one cell divided and joined with another to form a two-celled animal, each cell had to recognize and work with the other. With further additions of more, even billions, of cells, animals had to develop systems that would allow all kinds of cells to work together, and foreign cells to be eliminated or destroyed. This is the origin of the immune system.

We like to consider *natural law* as a derived extension of an individual immune system, which encodes instinctual behavior that successfully sustains an animal species. We do not have to canonize such principles as common decency in human interactions, because as adults, we instinctively know it. Only lives lived by intuition can bring us the certainty and effortless confidence required for fulfillment.

Intuition & Attitude

Much of our dysfunction and misery is the result of our failure, in the first two to three years of life, to attain separation from our parents, or to form feelings that we are deserving of our unique places in this world, with lives guided by intuition. Our senses of identity and individuality could not exist without the sense of intuition.

A dictionary definition of "attitude" is "manner, disposition, feeling, position, etc., toward a person or thing." The awareness of attitude is not ordinarily classified as being one of our senses, which normally include sight, sound, touch, taste, smell, and intuition, but attitude should be considered the seventh sense. We base our behavior toward others on what we sense to be their attitudes, and they reciprocally perceive our own projected attitudes about ourselves. Our attitudes broadcast how we feel about ourselves—our self-esteem or self-images. They publicly display what beliefs govern our behavior even when we're alone. Personal attitudes are evolving, developing feelings, which constitute the projected sum total of our self confidence, self-worth, our appraisals of our competence, our places in the pecking order of humans, and all of our adopted beliefs.

Attitude as the seventh sense differs from the other six senses in that it has two parts. The most outstanding aspect of attitude is that it represents the amalgamation of the first six senses, as they have supplied raw sensory data to our subconscious minds to form images. We project, as our personalities and attitudes, composites of these relative fixed images. Every animal in the world projects in this manner. We could liken it to the process of ultrasonography, where the machine both generates a sound wave signal, and interprets the sound waves that are reflected back to the sound generator. Our human brains automatically and instantly interpret the returning signals of our projections to give us the modes and feelings of others. This sensing of others indicates to us any permissive entrees for interaction and defines the limits of meaningful communication.

Attitude is our foremost presentation of ourselves to others. Simultaneously, we read the attitudes emanating from others, and they reciprocally read ours. In initial encounters, there may be considerable pretense and bravado, but when we add our intuitive attention to the incoming information, we can interpret the different signals and begin to communicate in more substantive ways.

If we want to know our whereabouts in social interactions, there is nothing more important than our awareness of attitudes of all individuals in our current association. The growth of our own personality awareness is necessary to allow ourselves to have diligent recognition of our own attitudes, as well as the projected attitudes of others. This seventh sense is basic for good communication and social interaction. Before we visit foreign countries, we study their customs and native languages. However, more important than spoken language is the appreciation of attitude, which is a universal common denominator. Knowing that all attitudes are age-related will allow us to better understand the level at which we can have meaningful communication. Immature, age-related attitudes are greater handicaps than limited knowledge of languages.

Attitudes determine basic behavior and all attitudes are age-related. It is important to know that when our bosses or fellow workers are behaving with attitudes of three-year-olds, we cannot communicate with them if our attitudes and expectations are at a four-year-old, or a more mature, level.

Attitudes determine behavior, and all elements are solidly bound to the ages at which they are adopted. The original defensive reactions and belief formations, which cause the adoption of attitudes, are more easily understood if we consider all behaviors to be normal and acceptable in specific age groups. Ninety-five percent of semi-permanent attitude formation is adopted in the first six years of life. The two major divisions in the formation of attitudes are infancy (birth to three years) and childhood (three to six years). In each grouping, there are normal and acceptable behaviors. Subsequently, when we are reacting defensively, we are reenacting fixed, learned behaviors. Each individual behavior exemplifies the age-related attitude. Long-term social interactions can only be successful when each participant intuitively considers the lowest common denominator of the age-related attitudes of the other individual.

The ringer is that we all can and do play adult most of the time. When we both are playing adult, we can amicably solve almost any common problem. When we pay attention, it is exceedingly easy to be aware, in a fraction of a second, when others become defensive and revert back to their protective age-related attitudes. But it is even more germane that we alert our awareness to our own automatic reversions to infantile or childish attitudes. Naturally, we all desire harmonious relationships, but all such striving will fall away under prolonged stress. Our basic attitudes about ourselves, with their accompanying hidebound behaviors, will keep us from pretending to be more than what we feel are our self-images and self-worth. Use of all of the seven senses is essential in order to know what we are bringing to social interactions and what is being contributed by those with whom we interact.

Managing Emotional Energy

Our emotional energy is limited as stringently as the number of hours we have in each day. How we manage that energy determines not only our emotional health, but, in large part, our physical health as well.

We budget our time to deal with the everyday necessities and obligations of our lives, often leaving little or no discretionary time for leisure and pleasure. Most of our time is spent eating, sleeping, and earning our livings, but to this must be added our travel time, time to take care of our children and families, and time to take care of ourselves.

Although, at first glance, it may seem that our time and energy are spent in just living, in all likelihood, we consistently use up most of our emotional energy by dealing with our anger about the past and our fear of the future. Little remains for meaningful interpersonal relationships. In reality, we can only truly live in this moment that is in the NOW, for the past is gone, and the future will never come, but if we consistently keep our emotions fixed on the past and the future, we cannot pay attention to the present, the NOW. The cost, both physical and emotional, of evading the present by attempting to live in the past and the future is very high and is at the root of half of physical diseases and nearly all emotional maladjustment.

Consider the following situation. Our parents are quarreling again, trading bitter insults, their voices raised in angry shouts. We overhear them as we lie nearby. What emotional message do we receive from our parents? As infants, we perceive our parents' anger as directed at us—we feel utterly rejected and that we are about to die. This is because our unconscious minds apply all emotion to ourselves. Helpless to attempt physical escape, we instinctively protect ourselves the only way we can—by withdrawing into ourselves to shut out these terrifying feelings. Being rejected when we are very young is tantamount to being threatened with losing our life support systems. It is perhaps the most painful, and certainly the most lasting, rejection that we can feel. These events are subconsciously remembered, and we unconsciously continue to recall them with underlying fear throughout our lives.

When we use up most of our emotional energy on the past and future, our personalities and our physiologies undergo profound changes. Turned inward, our emotional energy is transformed into preoccupation, indecisiveness, evasiveness, emotional withdrawal or "tuning out," anxiety, or depression. Turned outward, it becomes bitterness, resentment, irritability, argumentativeness, hatred, or violent temper. As anger or fear, it triggers a surge of adrenaline, tightens our muscles, sharpens our nerves, speeds up our heart rates, elevates our blood pressures, and, after an initial, sudden holding of breath, it boosts our respiration, while shutting down or suppressing our digestive and immune systems.

Every bit of the past that we reenact—and that we want to be different from what it actually was—drains our emotional energy. Rage, anger, and all the derivatives of anger—resentment, hate, sullenness, and vengefulness—drain our emotional energy as surely as mortgage, rent, or car payments drain our incomes. The fears we harbor, whether deeply buried, subtle, or profoundly overt, use up our emotional energy as surely as night-lights or electric stoves use up electricity. Anger and fear burn up our emotional energy by keeping us in constant readiness for dangers that are long past or only imagined. The more emotional energy we use up, the less we have left for communicating, listening to others, and expressing love, affection, and esteem, and the less of us is available to our children, spouses, friends, and extended families.

We can all intuitively appreciate attitude, that is, how much emotional energy and openness we feel radiating from others, and, at any given moment, how others behave towards us. When we detect a degree of approval or warmth in someone, we may describe that person as being affable or as having charisma. We are also aware of aloofness or antipathy on the part of others, which we are likely to interpret as lack of interest in us or hostility toward us as individuals. We sense another's attitude and can determine when someone has time for us or when he is, in effect, telling us to, "Get lost." If, in the second case, someone is reacting in anger to his past or caught up in fears of the future, then the apparent rejection may have little or nothing to do with us. Nevertheless, we are likely to feel that his actions are personally directed toward us, and we feel advised not to come too close.

Anger and fear instantly mobilize our bodies' defenses, preparing us for immediate life or death struggles—for "fight or flight." Our most primitive defensive force, anger, expressed as rage, operates essentially at the level of the midbrain and brain stem; it short-circuits the long neuronal connections to the cortex and the higher centers of the central nervous system. The more intense our anger, the more our actions become mindless defenses, devoid of any higher intellectual consideration. We direct our anger at offending persons or objects, but the chief psychological and physiological effects are felt by us as direct wear and tear on our bodies.

Although anger's immediate purpose is to get us to fight—to repel, disable, or kill our attackers—its ongoing and prevailing purpose is to control others, or at least get them to do something for us. Our angry crying as newborn infants ensures that our caretakers notice us and that our needs to be fed or warmed or held are immediately met. If our parents delay, our infant anger will turn to rage. When the delay is repeated again and again, that rage will become fixed as an emotional defense. For our lifetimes, the more helpless we feel, the more we sense that the only way to get *respect* is by extracting it from our caretakers by the use of anger.

Between the ages of about two-and-a-half to six, when we are repeatedly ignored, rebuffed, or thwarted, we learn other emotional defenses based on the subtler forms of anger, such as fussiness, crankiness, resentment, and hatred. In each case, however, the purpose of anger is the same—to control others.

Anger can hurt, cripple, or kill us, slowly or all at once, and most of the time, that is exactly what it does. On rare occasions, however, and for the briefest periods, anger can also help us. Anger, by its nature, is our most primitive, ultimate, and instantaneously available life-saving mechanism. By nature's design, we can never lose this ultimate defense. When we, as older children or adults, have no alternative but to fight, anger can save our lives by numbing us to pain, and by giving us the strength and courage we need to defend ourselves, because it temporally overrides and prevents fear. It can goad us into needed activity and roust us out of self-pity, defeatism, or inertia. Anger can also help define personal limits that must be respected—for example, anger toward those who keep imposing on us, or come onto us uninvited or too strongly. However, in general, anger serves no useful or beneficial purpose in our interpersonal relationships.

The basic purpose of fear, on the other hand, is to control us—to get us to flee some threat, real or imagined. Unlike anger, fear always requires some degree of higher brain function. To be fearful, we must first picture an image of some threatening event in our minds and then use the defenses we have learned to avoid it. The hundreds of fears we keep in our minds, whether conscious or unconscious, place a constant drain on our emotional energy. Our fears are backed up by elaborate, lightning-quick defense systems held in constant readiness, and the cost to us, like the cost of our national defense budget, is enormous.

Emotional energy used to form and reinforce our resentments of the past and fears for the future is unavailable to us in our peaceful lives and sustained intimate relationships. Energy used to defend us against threats long past or an only imagined future is turned inward, and also expresses itself in inappropriate and often hurtful behavior toward others, most often family members. The misdirection of this energy thus serves as the chief cause of illness in our bodies and unhappiness in our personal relationships. This aggravated wear and tear on our bodies is responsible for perhaps one half of all physical diseases.

Through surgery and medication, standard medicine can repair most injuries to our bodies and correct many imbalances in our physiologies. Alternative medicine can help alleviate pain, muscle tension, and constipation. What we really need, however, is a therapy to address the basic causes of anger and fear—or better still, a system of teaching that will prevent anger and fear from being converted and fixed into energy-draining, life-diminishing, emotional defenses. *Full Share: Claiming Our Birthright to Energy, Growth, Love, and Fulfillment* describes the origins and perpetuation of anger and fear and their resulting defenses. We are born with anger, but with very few fears. The anger that we fail to outgrow in the normal emotional maturation process and the fears that we are forced to learn in childhood, we carry into adulthood. Our deep-seated emotional defenses and resentments are learned almost entirely from our caretakers. These defenses are formed to protect our individualities, and therefore, we are not likely to spontaneously undertake any remedial activity to release us from wanting the past to be different or to remove fear from the future. Therefore, our defenses will continue to shut down an emotional part of us—and therefore, a part of our lives. Throughout the world, in every family, town, city, and country, people use anger to dominate and control others.

We routinely squander our life energy. This book details the mechanism by which we arrived at this perilous condition and presents the knowledge of how we can free up our precious emotional resources. We must acknowledge the personality arrests in ourselves and others, bring formative events to consciousness, and use the light of adult wisdom to reframe and demystify them, so that they become mere memories rather than unconscious, controlling reactions. Only then will we be able to truly respond to life with all of our resources for our and others' benefit.

Power

There is a distinct difference between management and control; the distinction is in our attitudes and our intentions. When we are secure and confident in ourselves, this self-assurance gives us many options. We can manage ourselves, and we have the additional reserves to acknowledge the abilities of others and oversee their productive efforts. We can take pleasure as we recognize and assist each individual to accomplish his own goals as well as bringing everyone together to achieve a common goal.

When we are insecure, our attitudes are limited by fear, and then our options are few. We are prone to take strict control, feeling that we must incur little or no risk of the unknown. In general, the more we feel inadequate and insecure, the more we feel the need to control not only ourselves, but all others around us. The more we trust ourselves and other people, the more we can manage, with creative discernment, both our own and their productivity.

Fearfulness emanates from lack of belief in ourselves, in our self-images and our self-worth, and can be expressed in extremes of either too much activity, or no activity. If we are power hungry, fearfulness turns into aggressive and oppressive domineering.

Perhaps even more exasperating is the expression of these low self-images and timidity when we choose to use not direct control, but rather, manipulation by means of passive obstruction.

The epitome of a dictatorial person was Josef Stalin, who killed millions of Soviet citizens in his attempt to prevent anyone from acting in opposition to his personal beliefs. He behaved as if anyone with an attitude that differed from his was life threatening, and he also feared anyone who reasoned the same way he did, for they threatened him by competing with him. The other extreme of this spectrum of fearfulness is exemplified by the battered wife of an abusive alcoholic husband, who in her fear, behaves as if she has no power or right to assert her own individuality.

The manipulation of power in families can be magnified in industry and nations. A benevolent dictator can, for a while, run a company or nation most efficiently, because when all dissension and alternate ideas are suppressed by his organization, he can rule with few cross-purposes. However, in the long run, all such organizations collapse because of their lack of flexibility. Strict control will not tolerate any individual creativity. The mounting pressure of this inflexibility in the organization inevitability stimulates its members to become creative for their own sakes. They will divert their energy in attempts to "beat the system," and thereby divert the company's good to their own benefit and gain. The resulting corruption will eventually bring down the whole system.

Universally, people appreciate money as real power. Its power, however, is limited, because it can buy only approval for what we do or want; it cannot buy acceptance of us for *who we are.* The nouveau riche may pay for membership into the club, but this does not assure them that the other members will accept them as equals. This is expressed in the trite saying, "We can't buy love." Each of us has the sole proprietorship of that emotional part of ourselves that allows us to extend acceptance and esteem to others. Theoretically, this control should be entirely elective, but its spontaneity is limited by any and all of the fear images that we maintain as subconscious scenarios, causing automatic fear and defense or avoidance responses. These reactions are registered in the limbic parts of our brains and do not require cognitive thought for activation. The attitudes that embrace prejudice, bigotry, and hate are all perceived from past experiences and learned as derived values. Release from these limiting images can be accomplished only when we divest ourselves of fearfulness and are able to adjust and upgrade our attitudes about ourselves, our self-worth, and self-acceptance.

The seeking and exacting of power is a most damaging force that is employed by members of families or nations. Each individual's attempting to control the others exemplifies the most common expression of this power struggle in families. The two most commonly used devices are anger and argumentation. When we feel unworthy of esteem for being *who we are*, then we will seek respect to force an equalizing social position. The anger, or the threat of the use of anger, to produce fear, is designed to result in the capitulation of the victim. Anger is brutish, unfeeling power, used, allegedly, to create the *respect* that we demand. Anger's natural design is a universal device to force others to yield or change according to our own demands. In general, the more inadequate or ineffective we feel ourselves to be, the more we apply anger to control and take charge of others.

The worldwide prevalence of angry individuals is the single most common cause for these individuals experiencing limited options and, therefore, restricted quality of life. Solutions to world problems require thoughtful responses by people not controlled by their own anger.

Argumentativeness is an attitude of a four-year-old, and it serves as a protective emotional bulkhead. It is, in essence, the expression of subtle fear of loss of assumed control. To argue is to defend (perceived emotionally as ultimately for our lives' sake) any of our fixed beliefs and prejudices. When our identity is not secure, questioning of our beliefs is tantamount to rejection of us as individuals. There is a world of difference between discussion and argumentation.

Discussion is a mind stimulating exercise practiced by two or more people engaged in the quest of seeking further understanding and is often based on the desire to reach consensus. On the other hand, to take and defend an alleged justifiable or unjustifiable steadfast position is argumentation. Its very nature is adversarial, and argumentation has the single objective of domination by forcing our dogma onto others. In argumentation, the foundation and background of our beliefs is of no importance; we must inflict our views on others to be winners. This practice will result in the creation of two losers in our interpersonal relationships. By design and intent, argumentation is an entirely closed-minded encounter, in which there is an attempt to force and subjugate our adversaries with our dogma. In reality, we only need to argue when we are fearful of the foundation of our beliefs or of ourselves. Consequently, in adult behavior, when someone makes a statement which we wish to better understand, we question him. If the speaker, however, rather than explaining the foundation of his point view, begins to *defend* his belief, then instantly and automatically, his thinking mind is shut down, except to recruit new ammunition to attack us. Intuitively, we can instantly sense his attitudinal change—suddenly, we are adversaries. If we cannot immediately change the subject, we have the choice of walking away or engaging in a mindless battle for power.

Argumentation is an exercise between two people acting mindlessly in a power struggle, in which each is attempting to subjugate the other and force him to accept his personal dogma. All arguments have this basic pattern, which rightly belongs to four-year-old children devoid of intellectual concepts: "It is my turn." "It isn't." "It is my turn."

Our accumulated fears are the overwhelming impediments to achieving our maximally evolved emotional lives. Even though we subconsciously know, and gut feelings alert, we still persist in following old programs learned from parental examples. Unfortunately, argumentation is socially acceptable. It is a classic four-year-old behavior, an age-related personality arrest, and will ruin our marriages or at least make them unpleasant, unless one partner is routinely submissive and desires to live with an emotional four-year-old. Each time we argue in the presence of our children, we inoculate them with fear that instructs them to mindlessly stand up and defend themselves, right or wrong. When we transmit this family virus, we can reasonably predict that, as a consequence of our example, this display will restrict our children's achievements and close their minds as it has ours.

Probably the most lifelong damaging example of the use of fear is our routine use of anger to control our infants' behavior. On the surface, using anger, which infants perceive as life threatening, repeatedly to manipulate our babies' behavior can be an efficient device. Temporarily, it works so well. However, the long-term emotional damage can be horrendous. Small babies have no deep thoughts or sophisticated philosophy, but only intuitive awareness of those attitudes derived from the accumulated experiences of millions of ancestors who survived to procreate. The survival drive is shared in common with all newborn mammals. In nature's scheme, *acceptance is life, and rejection is death.* Anger used to control infants is the essence of rejection and amounts to a death threat, since infants sense that they will die if abandoned.

Even in adults, exposure to overt anger will produce discomfort, insecurity, or fear by inciting a desire to shut it out or get far away from the source. A common device for an angry, dictatorial person is to use pictorial imagery to envisage bad things happening if his wishes are not satisfied.

In contrast to managing by control is running a family or business by guiding and directing individual efforts for common purposes. Direction management is a powerful tool when done expertly, for it represents the combined effort of two or more people or forces. Historically, Lewis and Clark managed the most astonishing feat in 1802-1805 as they lead thirty-three men on a 6000-mile trek throughout uncharted wilderness, collected scientific data, and mapped the whole route. They returned home with the loss of only two men—one who probably died from a ruptured appendix, and another who deserted. This is an example of competent leaders uniting a group to achieve a remarkable and sustained activity based on the life affirming use of true power.

Victim

If we fail to establish strong identities during our first three years of life, we may forever after play the role of victim. We retain the attitudes about our places among other people, which initially, as children, are as absolute victims. Except for complaining cries, babies are helpless to do anything to correct unfavorable circumstances. Infants and small children have to cooperate with their caretakers to secure food, protection, and shelter. We fashion our attitudes about our self-worth and our relative rank in hierarchy among others in the human pecking order early. We accept as reality the cognitive thought that we, in our infantile states, have no power except to ingratiate ourselves to obtain some degree of acceptance.

When the need for acceptance fails to give us esteem for being our own persons, we accommodate our lives to varying degrees of rejection. When we sense that we are abandoned, we became aggressive. The only active device is to cry and writhe in anger. This infantile anger is an automatic attempt to get *respect*, that is, parity with dominance of other people. We demand attention in order to survive. Respect gives us a modicum of control over our caretakers.

Certainly, in this reality, our anger, especially when it is loud and prolonged with crying and thrashing about, gives us the power to force recognition. When we exercise this control hundreds of times, it becomes not only a habit, but an adopted attitude, because experientially this behavior is the only way to get respect and survive. In later infancy and early childhood, whining is a more subtle adaptation of this control maneuver. Unless we revise our early beliefs, we can spend the rest of our lives alternating between these two extremes; that of supplicating ourselves as victims, by sniveling, whining, complaining, and claiming unfairness, or, at the other end of the spectrum, attempting to assume supreme dominance through infantile anger and rage. The more impotent we believe ourselves to be, the more we use these two basic adjustments for our emotionally restricted lives.

Stifling Enthusiasm and Spontaneity

To an infant, love means that we fulfill his dependency needs, that is, we accept and support him, and create a safe place for him. As we fulfill these conditions, he can feel safe, and therefore, he will want to be with us. This is his response and expression of the infantile form of *love*. At all ages, the essence of love is acceptance.

It is impossible for a newborn infant to have and demonstrate an altruistic, adult form of love. An infant is so dependent and needy that he can go only with his instincts for survival. Accordingly, he expresses what he needs and wants. He categorically ignores any demands put upon him. He feels safe only where he is accepted as he is. Good intentions are of no value to him, unless they are accompanied by a caregiver's projected feelings of acceptance. A show of love from a well-intentioned sacrificing parent may be practically meaningless to the infant, unless that parent also conveys and projects an attitude of acceptance.

An insidious form of rejection is produced by a parent or grandparent who, to satisfy his own needs, cajoles that infant to produce specific performances, attitudes, or emotional responses. An adult who behaves in this supercilious manner does so in order to gain his own sense of accomplishment for having "taught" the baby a new stunt. The adult might have personal satisfaction in his accomplishment that is similar to what he might feel when he successfully trains his dog to fetch a stick.

Also, the need of the caretaker to get approval from the infant can blind him to the fact that a small infant cannot understand the parent's own need for approval. He can only feel relaxed and snuggle when his own dependency needs are satisfied.

Adults are not equal to babies in sensitivity and awareness. An infant is born with genetically governed survival instincts, which include intuitive understanding and an awareness of attitude, and this is his first language of communication. Initially, he responds only to stimuli received through his seven senses—sight, sound, touch, taste, smell, intuition, and attitude. He automatically understands, by and through his own intuition and keenness in reading attitudes. At the outset, the greatest guide is intuition, that is, his inborn ability to tune into and automatically respond to feelings generated by, and the attitudes projected by, all of those who attend him. For instance, simply holding an infant neither gives reassurance nor creates a safe place if the holders are tense, angry, or disinterested.

All through the first and second years, the normal infant is interested in everything about him and is eager to try any maneuver to manipulate all things and people that are within his capabilities. This is the normal exploratory state of the human animal, and this basic drive should be actively encouraged and sustained for each individual the rest of his life. This is nature's course, unless it is damped in infancy. Consider the consequences of losing or negating the state of curiosity.

Remember when we were children and played in mud puddles and their little rivulets. We could dam up the flow of water to direct the little streams downhill to almost any place, but we could not make the water run uphill. Similarly, when we tune into a child's energy and emotional drive, we can understand where he is headed. Figuratively, we can put dams to create diversionary channels to steer him away from danger to a safer place where he can achieve by learning from his exploration.

The two major mechanisms for thwarting curiosity and exploration are anger and attempted programming before the infant's nervous system is physiologically mature enough to accept thoughtful, corrective instruction. Returning to our mud puddle analogy, when a child reaches the age of two to three, he can intellectually perceive that he has the ability to take water up hill in a bucket to create his own stream. Then he is old enough to accept some directions from a person outside of himself. Before that age, only single command words are processed. All complicated instruction can only confound and confuse an infant. Some children at age two-and-a-half and most at age three years can begin to reason and compare. Most importantly, if the child has not already been emotionally crippled, he will assume a sense of responsibility. This maturation marks the boundary between infancy and childhood. In infancy, only diversionary tactics can be administered without risking permanent damage to enthusiasm for exploration. When given unlimited choices and his own testing, he needs the right to learn by making mistakes.

A child without mandated limits is a holy terror and later can become an uncouth, uncontrollable adult. A parent's job is to delineate the safe place, in which the child can feel free to experiment and reasonably express himself. The size of this arena needs to be progressively increased all the way to adulthood, where conventional limits become the bulwark ordered by society. Diversionary dams to safely channel a child's behavior and emotional expression are the best method to enforce boundaries. To occasionally enforce these boundaries with a whack to the butt causes no more lasting damage or future problems than that of the child bumping his shins in play. Quite in contrast is the enduring emotional trauma and damage caused by his caretakers' controlling by anger. Minor physical trauma is part of living and is soon forgotten. Anger and rage mean only one thing to an infant, that is, life-threatening, utter rejection. A reminder by a whack on the butt is merely calling attention to a boundary limit, like the scraping of a knee on the wall when we get too close. As a matter of fact, every minute of every day, each living animal is subjected to physical limits in his immediate environment. Failure to adjust to these limits will keep us continuously uncomfortable and bruised. However, such parental reminders as a whack on the butt must be delivered completely free of anger or resentment. Anger and control have but one clear message for us, that is, *rejection for being the persons we are*. Anger and rejection cause permanent emotional scaring, making the child fearful of getting too close to the parent.

Not until the age of two-and-a-half to three will the child be able to conceive of the concept of *not doing*. Before that age, the infant has a perception of *do*, but not of *not do*. The negative command is totally ineffective, because the infant's brain has not yet matured to have sufficient functioning synaptic neuronal connections to be able to process the changing of a negative to a positive. The mental gymnastics of converting a negative into a positive injunction requires the considerable function of adult neocortical brain function. The child's muscles can respond only to a positive command. His subconscious mind can only do and defend. The subtle part of his brain is totally devoid of any *negative defense*–he cannot picture a negative defense. Can he draw the image of *Not Doing* whatever? Even adults respond much better to positive instructions, because the unconscious mind spontaneously moves toward images. If we hear, "Don't think of a pink elephant," what do we begin to picture?

An all too common technique is for Mother to add anger to her ordinary speaking voice, "Don't do that!" A young infant understands no words; his communication is by understanding projected intuition and attitude. Mother will almost surely get an immediate reaction when she frightens (to perceived death by rejection) the child by adding *anger* to her voice command. By exuding anger or rejection in her attitude, she frightens the infant into submission and obedience. Infants can respond to such positive command as, "Stop," "Wait," and a little later in infancy, "No-no," as long as these commands are free of emotionally charged anger. As the months go by, the infant progressively acquires a more developed nervous system, whereby he can process such commands as, "Do not do that," as long as they are delivered free of anger or resentment.

An infant is interested only in satisfying himself.

When we require a baby to perform any act that he does not initiate, we may well accomplish directing his action, but at a cost of reducing, or at least to some small part, compromising, his natural energy and enthusiasm. Emotionally, the needier we are as parents, the more likely we will be to attempt to program "My Child" into performing to satisfy us and to assert ourselves as commanders. A most common command may be, "Give mama a kiss."

We will love and desire to be with the one who accepts us for who we are. We will be repelled by the needy person who attempts to buy our affection in the name of love, expressed as doing a service act for us.

Our spontaneity and enthusiasm will continue to serve us our whole lives if they are allowed to flow unhindered in our infancy and childhood.

Central Nervous System and Our Dark Side

The human brain is the product of millions of years of evolution. The one-celled animal developed an immune system in order to become a two-celled animal, and later, a multi-celled creature. The immune system allowed each cell to recognize its fellow as friendly and necessary. Life's next big jump in development was arranging a nervous system that would accommodate all the various parts of the body and coordinate their functions.

Over eons of time, the central nervous system evolved. Only after the acquisition of the rudimentary nervous system, did animals develop the bony skull and vertebral column for protection of the central nervous system, that is, the spinal column and brain. The central nervous system has three parts: First, and most primitive, is the reptilian brain. The second part is the limbic brain, and third is the mammalian brain, also known as the neocortex. We acknowledge these segments because, as animals evolved, so did their capabilities in performance and their complicated defense mechanisms.

The reptilian brain, which is located in the brainstem, operates in the present and can acquire only limited learning experiences. The primary function of the reptilian brain is to assure survival by the aggressive use of brute force and sex. The reptilian brain has no future or past; it simply responds to the current stimuli with behavior patterns that are encoded in the DNA.

The limbic brain, which operates as the midbrain, has the acquired ability to accumulate and store images of the immediate past. With these images of successful survival, it develops reaction and habit patterns, which become conjoined with coordinated defenses. Also, the evolving limbic brain marks the beginning of the acquisition of the development of minor ability to delay and to elect behavior from its store of learned reactions. The limbic brain has little or no perspective of the future, but reacts automatically to genetically encoded behavior and its previously recorded learned imagery and acquired habits and skills.

The mammalian brain, the neocortex, is capable of comprehending not only the present, but also the past and the future. With this added perspective, an individual can project probable and possible outcomes of various courses of action. A human being has the maximum range of choice and can put himself into the most desirable places possible, should he choose to use his neocortex. In addition to new and increasing choices, he can elect to automatically duplicate or veto repeating past behavior. He can synthesize prospective images of new experiences and learning. Critical judgment and intellect are the highest forms of past achievement, allowing man to make comparative evaluations of the relative merits of alternatives. The neocortex always depends on the limbic brain to supply intuitive fragments from which the neocortex can assemble innovative, new imagery. However, these synthesized, new images need millions of details which must be filled in by the subconscious mind.

When we review man's cultures, philosophies, and religions, we must consider the extremes of light and darkness, good and evil. A categorization can be drawn for the behaviors of man being virtuous or devilish. If man is basically saintly, then we should bring out his best points. Or, if he is basically sinful, as suggested in Calvinism, then we should do everything to control and prevent his evil countenance from being able to rule him. From our study of people, we know that every person has already been at one of these two extremes and potentially can be at the other. When we are born into this world, we start out with dreadful behavior. The challenge is whether or not we outgrow this infantile, emotional behavior and mature beyond brutishness.

When we consider mankind exhibiting the dark side, we must look at the behavior of a single human. As he satisfies his wants and appetites, this fellow is totally lacking in consideration for others, because he does only what will immediately please him. When he is angry, he uses his anger by primarily demanding that others do his bidding and accede to his dictates. He strikes out, flailing his arms in every direction, indiscriminately hitting whomsoever he can. He makes no attempt to control his elimination and soils his environment. Whatever he can lay his hands on, he takes without permission. He has no love for anyone—only a desire to satisfy his dependency needs. Obviously, I am describing "us" as we were during our first year of life. None of these traits are vile or wrong; they are just infantile–primitive and normal for the lowest animal forms. Merely aging and growing physically do nothing to help us outgrow our infantile attitudes and their correlative behaviors. Even developing intellectually will not, by itself, overcome these undesirable traits. In fact, they will be heightened by the sophistication of antisocial behavior to make us not only more effective, but much more harmful. When we are placed in intimidating situations or under personal strain, even though we are temporarily capable of performing in a cultured manner, we will, lacking emotional growth, behave by acting out these infantile traits that are only understandable in a normal baby.

Here is a strange dichotomy: On one hand, we recognize that an individual who is arrested in his intellectual development in infancy will, at best, always behave as an idiot or an imbecile. On the other hand, we fail to acknowledge that the person who is emotionally arrested in infancy will be a moral and behavioral social disaster. The difference is that, even with intensive training, an idiot or imbecile cannot pass as an adult with a normal mentality. But, quite in contrast, the emotionally arrested person has the capacity and intellect to choose, if he is not harried, to falsely present himself as a responsible adult.

When we allow a living thing to develop to its own best form, whether it is a tomato plant, a Hampshire hog, or a human being, it will develop into a fine representative of its own species. In order to cultivate or equip a representative of any species, we must give this individual protection in a safe space to be cultured or nurtured. As a society, we do an increasingly fine job of providing our babies with good nutrition, immunization, and shelter, so that our children grow to be physically strong and vigorous. We emphasize Head Start, intellectual stimulation, and enriched education to cultivate their minds. But as a society, we do a fair to wretched job in supporting our babies with a caretaking attitude that projects *acceptance of them as equal separate human beings.* This support is essential to enable them to reach their own full potentials of growth in their emotional development.

There is every indication that when a parent knowledgeably and emotionally supports his infant with the attitude that his child is separate and equal, the baby will grow up feeling emotionally adequate as a whole, unflawed person. This parental attitude affords the necessary support and assurance for the child to automatically mature into the adult he is genetically designed to be. Natural emotional growth results in full adulthood, which is characterized by warmth, openness, and acceptance. Attainment of any other attitude, with its attendant behavior, indicates that emotional growth was stunted. A flawed emotional development is the most likely result of intense or prolonged exposure to dysfunctional parental interpersonal attitudes and behaviors. Philosophically, as adults, we may argue about the degree of importance that the threat of non-acceptance has on the infant, but we believe that, to an infant, perception of all forms of rejection are tantamount to death threats. Acceptance equals living and rejection equals death. When we are very young, we cannot be non-reactive or indifferent. When we sense that our lives or our individualities are being threatened, we will sell our souls to survive.

When we consider the whole of evolution since the earth was formed, we need to be ever mindful that all animals have much of the same basic genetic material in each cell of their bodies. Embryologically, each of us starts with the basic reptilian nervous system. This wonderfully organized bundle of nervous tissue first evolved to be simply reactive, devoid of any thoughtful considerations. It is designed to automatically react to its environment, and therefore survive and procreate. This basic behavior is encoded and directed by the DNA. This involuntary survival drive regulates the body's vital functions. As humans, we have retained this ancient basic hard wiring; any and all refinement and sophistication are simply added to it.

Millions and millions of years after the organization of the reptilian brain, the limbic brain, located anatomically in the midbrain region, evolved. This midbrain area houses the subconscious mind, which, with its electronic machinery, regulates complex emotional reactions and social behaviors, and stores emotional experiences coupled with fear and defenses to form learned habits. These secondary functions were impossible with only a reptilian brain. In many more millions of years, humans and other higher animals developed the neocortex or rational brain, which gives us the ability to deliberate and make choices to alter our behavior. The neocortex can veto some or all of the power of two lower centers of the nervous system. However, this special power is temporarily abolished if we feel threatened to the point that automatic defenses are stimulated.

The problem is that at birth, the reptilian part of the nervous system is fully hooked up and operating. The limbic brain is somewhat operative, but the rational brain has only its hardware in place, which consists of billions of nerves. Synaptic connections are yet to be fully assembled, and sophisticated software programs are yet to be installed.

Infantile behavior is not vile or vicious; it is just the normal, basic, survival behavior of all lower animals, designed by nature and successfully tested billions and quadrillions of times to assure the survivable of the fittest. True so-called "human behavior" cannot begin to be dominant until much of the brain is fully hooked up and is self-programmed by learning through exposure to wholesome experiences.

At birth, the software start-up program is almost a direct holdover from the reptilian brain, which is fully adequate to sustain our survival through our birthing. The software for the limbic brain is in the early stages of organization and is operating poorly. The cognitive brain is years away from any programming. The software for the two higher centers must be developed as the nervous system is being put together electrically. This programming has a major built-in governing component engraved in our encoded genetic template that provides a traced outline of what the fully emotionally evolved human should be.

These directions are similar to the engraved template for the developmental directions of a cat, for they will govern the cat's social and mating behavior. Our emotional development follows a human template, and human emotional development is so complex that it can be moderated, diverted, or even arrested by the exposure to noxious life experiences and hazards during the first years.

Our emotional responses and behavior as newborns and infants will be standard as observed in all races throughout the world. A neonate's start-up attitudes and behavior represent generic survival traits, which can be characterized as "the dark side of man." As parents, our duty and obligation is to create safe places, protected and nurtured environments for our infants' emotional development, enabling them to outgrow this primitive phase of life.

In early infancy, we are forced to adopt the familial attitude of self; it is a matter of survival. We adopt these feelings long before we are prepared to do so wisely. The choosing and discriminating functioning of our infantile brains is handicapped, because initially, our central nervous systems are only partially connected.

Emotional growth, like physical growth, is often stunted. This occurs when one or more of our normal streams of energy is forced to shut down or is diverted. The stronger these inborn emotional streams are, the stronger will be our drive to be accepted as we are. Parts of the innate drive for acceptance and individuality consist of the need for freedom of expression, curiosity, inventiveness, assertiveness, industry, and exploration. The emotional part of this need, acceptance, is met by being consistently held affectionately, with warmth, by our parents.

When, in the first three years of life, any of these emotional streams are shut down or partially stifled, we will not be able to develop our complete identities. Our inborn senses of self-acceptance will be displaced by weak or poor self-images. Without strong self-images, we will not be able to realize our full creativity. Serious behavioral problems represent distortions or blockages—attitudinal bulkheads. The dark side of man, therefore, is the continuance of infantile behaviors at adult ages, at which time they are out of place and destructive to society.

Behavior, DNA, and Beliefs

The key to truly knowing a person is learning all we can about his past behavior. Behavior is the main stream of evidence about how we live our lives from beginning to end. Our various behaviors identify our attitudes, which, in turn, are age-related. The analysis of the historical track of our behavior portrays whatever base level we have established for ourselves and actively demonstrates our confidence in our individualities.

Except in a brain-damaged individual, all behaviors are normal human behaviors; for a very definable age group, a given behavior has a more or less standard occurrence. In order to make sense and communicate with another person, we need to first evaluate the setting of any given behavior. We must determine if he is behaving in a relaxed, tense, or impaired manner. His behavior is most revealing when he is preoccupied, for then his defenses are strictly subconscious and free of any pretense. Whenever and however he is behaving defensively and fearfully demonstrates that he feels his individuality is threatened. No one needs to defend any attitude or behavior that simply demonstrates who he truly is, that is, his self-image. As long as that self-image is in accordance with the template encoded in his DNA, he has no stress. He is himself. His full, natural life is characterized by relaxed self-acceptance, intuition, and true spontaneity.

Defense of our physical lives and safety is different from emotional defense, which is the protecting of our individualities, including our identities and self-images. To voluntarily give someone information about us or our behavior is entirely apart from defending details about ourselves. If the other person will not listen to valid information, he has the problem; we don't. If both of us are on the defensive, then we both have age-related attitude arrests. All defenses are learned reactions to the past and all are related to the behaviors appropriate to the ages at which they were formed.

Our attitudes regulate our behavior in interactions with other people and eventually determine our quality of life and our experiences. Also, for our continuing emotional growth, we must identify our own age-related attitudes and take complete and total responsibility for them before we can ever change.

Our attitudes are ruled by our belief systems. Our minds are the directors, which form, manage, and adjust our attitudes, but cannot forcefully control the formation and revision of our beliefs. Only resumption of normal maturation, which will be in conformity to the template that is in our DNA, can upgrade our attitudes and self-esteem. Our minds' job is to manage emotional energy, so our bodies are protected from our own energy turned inward, which would activate and energize our defense systems unnecessarily.

There are at least two basic driving forces in individual development. First, *Spirit* is the energy that holds us together as continuous entities from birth to death. Even as our minds develop or deteriorate and our physical bodies go through continuous changes, spirit is immutable. We experience spirit as the sense of existence in the moment.

Second, *DNA* is the one essential component of all life forms. This code for proteins distinguishes the individual and manifests the biological life force that drives survival and the procreation of the species. *Evolution is the drive to fulfill the genetically encoded potential of the DNA* and is the weaker force and creates our life's challenge. Ultimately, for the quality of life, this force is the most important. At the moment of inception, the templates encoded in our genes give us preordained developmental potentials. Any deviation from our paths due to the assumption of distorted self-images will make us emotionally dysfunctional.

In infancy, the first drive must be satisfied before we can be ourselves and fulfill our preordained potentials. Any self-effacing compromise of our identities (souls) needs to be differentiated from the voluntarily assumption of temporary roles to adjust and accommodate to circumstances, individuals, or groups with which we may associate.

Ideal human life, therefore, consists of the continuous sense of extending itself, spontaneously geared to maintaining its existence, procreation as a biological imperative, and the unadulterated full expression of our unique DNA potentials through perception, behavior, and emotion. These are the individual, intuitive, guided life paths contained in our DNA.

Emotional Responses

Our emotional reactions to life situations are determined by our beliefs and expectations. We alone create our feelings, whether they are good, bad, funny, disastrous, rewarding, or whatever. Two definable assumptions we have about ourselves—our self-images and our self-portraits—create the boundaries of our emotional responses. Our self-images represent our established feelings about our identities and our self-worth. Early in infancy and childhood, we semipermanently fix our assumptions, which define these viewpoints. When, early in our lives, we adopt attitudes about ourselves, they will be reenacted as if they are the reality of our self-worth. To adjust these basic attitudes requires guidance, desire, and effort.

At the opposite end of our ultimate baseline are our active fantasies, that is, our self-portraits. These self-portraits are wishful, depicting and projecting how we would like ourselves to be and how we would like others to view us. When our expectations are in keeping with our self-images, we will have very few disappointments, because we see our lives the way they are in relationship to our being. When our expectations are based on our self-images, we may well have joy and high moments, especially when we get more or a better deal than we anticipated. However, when we have received more than we feel we deserve, we may become uncomfortable enough so that the good feelings will soon be dissipated or lost, perhaps through our own sabotage.

When our expectations are determined by our self-portraits, our lives can be full of great temporary happiness, but more commonly, we will experience great disappointments because of unfulfilled, unrealistic expectations.

Fantasy and magical thinking are normal when we are emotionally arrested at about the age of three, and this will result in repeated disappointments. Superstitions, omens, lucky charms, mathematical systems, and fate will all influence our daily expectations. These mystical influences will weigh in heavily in determining our "luck." Without the magical thinking of a three year-old, the lottery, serious gambling, some religions, and most get-rich-quick scams could not exist.

As we analyze a person and become well acquainted with his individual behavior, appreciating both his self-image and his self-portrait, then we can recognize the mode in which he is momentarily operating. Much of the time, his emotional responses may be predictable. More importantly, his behavior will be understandable. The more rigid his beliefs and the more set his expectations, the more predictable will be his emotional responses.

Serious Emotional Disorders

Throughout the whole world, there is a standard emotional evolution comparable to the standard physical development of the human body. Accordingly, impeded emotional development reflects incrementally specific, maximum coping mechanisms for fending off life-threatening assaults and devastation to our individual identities. During the first six years, veritably all learned, basic, lifesaving defenses and personal attitudes are set in place for life. Most significant of all are those acquired in early infancy, and decreasingly so up to the age of three. In our early months of life, we form life's most important attitudes about our self-images, our self-worth, and our self-esteem. Unfortunately, we are forced to reflexively adopt vital attitudes when our brains have little or no ability to contemplate or use discerning judgments. In other words, at that early age, we lack adult perspective. With our infantile, "half-baked" brains, we determine what amended personas we will adopt for the rest of our lives. That is, unless we revise them.

After the age of six, our attitude adjustments are done mainly by synthesizing, building-up, and compounding those beliefs that we have already formed in previous experience. All the threatening encounters that we have before our brains and nervous systems are fully operating cause us to automatically form the best coping mechanism of which we are capable at that time. Later in life, we can change and emotionally "grow-up" progressively, but this growth does not happen routinely or automatically. Each time we allow ourselves to "act-out," we strengthen the attitudes that cause us to reenact immature behaviors. Overcoming any of the serious personality arrests of infancy is possible, but difficult, and we will probably need supporting groups and informed guides.

The serious emotional disorders stemming from infantile personality arrests include reliance on anger to control and get respect, career-homelessness, criminal behavior, marked obesity, inordinate slovenliness, drug addiction, alcoholism, domestic violence, fear, lack of intimacy, and isolation. Each of these disorders has specific and characteristic behaviors, each with its own definite pattern. These behavioral traits are age identifiable, as each trait arises in an infant normally, and should be exhibited maximally only at that age in which it occurs as standard and acceptable. A given cluster of traits, which occur normally at a definite developmental age, characterizes each given syndrome of seriously emotionally disabled persons.

Much of the time, severely emotionally dysfunctional individuals, with much determination and continuous effort, can and do behave in a reasonable, social manner. However, when they are under stress, or are incapacitated by illness or drugs, the pretense of emotional adulthood is automatically terminated, and they instantly revert back to their very early defenses, behaving in exactly the same ways that they did originally as small children. In these reenactments, they are repeating and exhibiting the same symptomatic traits that are typical of that age period when their emotional traumas first occurred and caused the emotional arrests. Emotional traumas have commensurate defenses for specific ages.

When we establish coping defenses that successfully save our lives hundreds of times, we will not be able to wish them away or supplant them willfully. When we sense that our lives or our identities are at stake, we can seldom countermand learned and practiced defenses. The very best we can do is to inhibit or blunt their obvious, immature attitudes and behaviors. Logically, we can know that substitute behaviors would be more fitting and potentially more rewarding, but without increased understanding, practice, and support, nothing will change our ultimate behaviors. Any lasting changes or alterations in our behavior must be done by emotionally resetting our attitudes about ourselves and revising the specific beliefs forming our self-images. For lasting changes in our adjustments to life, treatment must include changes in our perceptions of the past and our attitudes for the future.

The fact is that virtually all individuals with serious emotional problems can, at times, or even most of the time, act responsibly in an adult manner. However, they temporarily accomplish this by putting themselves under the constant stress of pretending that they are adults, forcing themselves to act in keeping with their self-portraits. These charades are meant to cover over their beliefs and feelings of inadequacy. However, when they perceive that they are abruptly threatened in their pretenses of being emotionally secure, their charades will dissolve. As their covers are blown, they will behave as dictated by their basic beliefs about themselves, with the age-related defenses mandating their behavior.

Behavioral Aspects of Psychiatric Problems

Antisocial Personality, Including the Criminal Mind Set

Antisocial people have traits in common, including impulsiveness, irresponsibility, amorality, and the inability to forego immediate gratification. They cannot form enduring affectionate relationships with others, yet their charm and plausibility may be highly developed. For limited periods of time, this skillful charm can be used for their own ends. In balance, their antisocial behavior shows little foresight and is not associated with remorse or guilt. They have little tolerance for frustration. Their anger can lead to serious hostility. This is a perfect description of individuals performing in adult bodies, but doing so with infantile attitudes and behaviors, which would indicate the formation of multiple emotional arrests in the developmental period from birth to two-year-old level. No one thinks it odd or alarming when infants care only for their own needs, regardless of the effect on others, but when adults behave in that way, they are criminals.

Borderline Personality

Borderline people can have some or all of the personality arrests found in the antisocial personalities, but, in addition, they have traits that are typically found in older infants at the two- to three-year-old level. In this developmental time period, children are still struggling to establish identities as separate individuals. While they are seeking to gain separateness and identity, they can be blocked in developing their emotional maturity. They react by forming protective bulkheads at the two- to three-year-old level. When arrested at that juncture, they are confused and unsure of their self-images. Although characteristically, they may remain unsure as to their identities, they usually have very definite and fixed notions of what they want and how others should behave. Their conceptions of the meanings of single words are fixed. Their reactions to the feelings of others can be total or absent. They have increasing imaginations and fantasies (magical thinking) about their everyday lives. These fantasies can be as strong as their rudimentary concepts of reality.

When children are caught in this part of their development, problems originate in severely dysfunctional families, which can force them to adopt coping skills that successfully keep some of their integrity alive. They form temporary emotional bulkheads to retain some degree of integrity about themselves by stabilizing and holding onto their current beliefs about their identities. Already, for themselves, they have established small, relatively safe places emotionally at this developmental period. Later, they cannot abandon those places, even though their immediate need for protection has long ceased to exist. Under stress, they return emotionally to these safe sanctuaries under their protective bulkheads, where they may now act out and play the childish games that they learned initially. This plays out in borderline personalities as making others responsible for their every feeling, and in threatening self harm to control others.

Depression

Depression is usually temporary. It is composed of a group of behavioral traits that recur following affronts by situational stress. This syndrome is a protective device that is reenacted when people are overwhelmed by stimuli that logically require action or commitment. It is a learned emotional refuge, because it represents a return to a safe place for the reenactment of a group of defensive traits characteristically found in deeply troubled infants of about thirty months of age. Historically, these infants have matured emotionally to about the age of two-and-a-half years. Then a stream of their development is blocked by the formation of bulkheads to protect their previously acquired emotional growth. Logically, these formations should be temporary devices. After the clearing of the temporary overload of turmoil caused by the current situation, they are no longer needed.

The most salient behavioral features of the depression syndrome include indecisiveness, hopelessness, helplessness, low self-image, lack of confidence, crying spells, loss of energy, and loss of feelings for others. These attitudinal traits affect bodily functions and can cause problems, such as sleep and eating disturbance and general slowing of body motion.

In doing age reenactment sessions, also called age regressions, with patients who experience depression, we find a common theme, in that patients share common experiences at the time in early childhood when they developed this special defensive, protective syndrome. It was at about two-and-a-half years of age. The common theme is that the dysfunctional caretakers created extraordinary stress or a family crisis. The sensitive children, at the age of about thirty months, were aware of the tremendous emanations of feelings and emotions; they sensed and reacted to the reception of all of these disturbing stimuli. They were aware that something needed to be done, but didn't know what. They were just at the age where their senses of responsibility were beginning to kick in. Nobody had the patience to interactively communicate with them or the ability to understand them.

At this age their coping abilities were limited. Their best responsive device was to shut themselves down in two ways. First, they blocked incoming harmful emotional emanations, and secondly, they overrode and stifled their own feelings. With these shut downs, they reactively retarded their physical actions, preventing them from doing something "wrong." These were their first depressions. Recurrent depressions are evidence of the reenactment of this protective device.

Depression is a life saving technique designed by nature to see children through early stressful periods. In future years, when again they perceive a situation that may overwhelm their two-year-old coping skills, they have ready, learned defenses which have successfully enabled them to live through previous similar crises. Also, this behavior is like that of infants, who have no concern for their future good.

Posttraumatic Stress Disorder

Patients with posttraumatic stress disorder have recurrent episodes of reexperiencing traumatic events, numbed emotional responsiveness, and dysphoric general hyperarousal. The central feature is reexperiencing trauma, which may occur as a wakeful nightmare reliving of a past traumatic event. This revivification is in the present tense. Patients may have chronic anxiety, hyper alertness, and insomnia, and may also be emotionally labile, irritable, restless, and tremulous, with occasional bursts of explosive anger and violent behavior. Many are less responsive to other people, events, and their usual pursuits.

Flash backs are like nightmares while we are awake. Emotionally, they have the same purpose as dreams, which is to perpetuate, without alteration, our self-images and belief systems. [See "The Purpose of Dreams" in *Full Share*.] Our subconscious minds have no time lines; everything is in the present—it's all happening now. This has to be so, because in order for our defense reactions to be life saving, they must be activated in milliseconds; we need to save our lives this instant.

Our subconscious minds are not subject to direct commands, but, rather, are activated by imagery. Dreams in man and in other mammals are necessary so that, nightly, we are obliged to review and reinforce our self-images. We do this by conjuring up images that emotionally stimulate the defenses and beliefs that constitute our self-images. The nightmares are especially important for revivification of past peril, which stimulates fear and thereby reinforces reenactments of already well-formed evasive defenses. This design primarily makes sure that we forever avoid those dreaded past predicaments.

Posttraumatic stress disorder starts with images, which initiate reenactment of traumatic experiences. The most disabling fears and anxieties have their origin in early childhood, because at this time, imagery and fantasy are foremost in the brain's development. In dreams, the specific imagery of locations and acting characters has no significant importance by itself. The important property of the images is their ability to stimulate and refresh our defense systems, causing them to be aroused and reinforced. Neither the identities of the actors nor the places are important, because only the dream imagery stirs the emotions. The purpose of dreams is to stimulate and practice our defense readiness, as well as to reinforce how we feel about ourselves.

Of those who are subjected to severe combat trauma or emotional upheaval, only a few develop posttraumatic stress disorder. Individuals must have had infantile or childish personality arrest profiles long before the traumas in combat. Subsequent exposure in combat caused the development of posttraumatic stress disorder. We will find that before the adult traumas, these individuals were emotionally immature and had very limited coping skills. The last traumas did not cause their breakdowns, but rather, only reactivated and intensified personality arrests that they had from infancy. Only prior propensity can explain fully that, given the same trauma, some individuals manifest posttraumatic stress disorder and others do not. The roadmap of serious emotional disorders is based on the understanding that all adult dysfunctional behavior results from basic defenses enacted in infancy and childhood.

Domination Contest

Whenever we want something from another individual, we put that person or animal in charge of us. The most common example of this truth is found in spoiled children. Looking at their development, we can understand the dynamics. This is the common scenario: Mother, even when she was a little girl, had very little self-identity as a separate individual in her own right, but got her orientation from what others thought and expressed about her. She was the classic nice little girl whose sense of being and self-worth demanded seeking approval from her peers and betters. She put her energy into continuously striving to conduct herself in the proper way at the appropriate time and thereby, got her sense of worth by being politically correct. When she married, she attempted to be the nice wife, and thereby, got her identity through pleasing her husband. When her baby was born, she devotedly transferred the bulk of her emotional energy to her child, and thereby, got her sense of worth through servicing her baby. She progressively transferred her expectations for her emotional support from family to husband to new baby. She now expects and desperately needs her baby's approval and love, responding to his every wish in an attempt to make him totally dependent on her. He becomes the spoiled child.

In this continuing precarious situation, she dares not do anything that might in any way displease her baby, lest her infant not love her, or even worse, reject her. She is now in peril, for when the child matures and Mother continues to put this unreal expectation on him to take responsibility for her emotional well being, he will resent and reject this role, which, from birth, he has been constantly unable to fill. As a result, he may predictably choose to leave and forsake Mother, except for brief appearances to fulfill perfunctory obligations. The spoiled child is not over-loved, but rather over-solicited. The parent then needs constant approval from the child to maintain any sense of self-worth, and thus, is totally dependent on the child.

When two individuals are behaving in adult mode, they create an opportunity for mutual expectation, accommodation, and affection, making this the basis of a workable marriage, because their interactions are free from power manipulation when neither spouse is needy. However, if a relationship is formed without this reciprocal adult sense of responsibility, this void creates a contest for power. The partner who is domineering may delude himself into feeling he is the winner, but in reality, both are losers, for each feels unfulfilled. Even in a quiet home free of argumentation, each may want or need something from the other, be it grocery money or sexual favor. Just as in work or business, the one who controls the money controls the power, and when someone has something we need, he controls us.

In the contest for domination, argumentation and anger virtually make discussion and adjustment impossible are, and both are "no brainers." The use of anger is an infantile emotional hang-up, and argumentation is a four-year-old emotional hang-up. Both are struggles for power. The use of either one of these devices precludes the use of our cognitive brains.

During the last ten years of active medical practice, Ted was employed by the Arizona Department of Corrections at the state penitentiary in Tucson. Because he had many years of experience in medicine, it was a great place to work, but the real fascination was the diversity of advanced games the inmates played to manipulate their environment. Ted became a fast learner in acquiring the faculty to stay on top of these arch manipulators. These criminal players were lifelong professional veterans, whose whole sense of fulfillment was to beat the system and constantly challenge any authority, including the doctor.

One of the most potentially dangerous games was played between the inmates and the prison guards. The inmates would select and befriend a guard who craved attention. They would make jokes and listen to his stories about life and his family. In other words, they would manipulate this guard so that he would want devoted attention and audience from the inmates. Once the guard got into this obligatory position, the prisoners knew that he was vulnerable and would be willing to do some things, such as smuggling out letters or bringing in contraband, including drugs.

In his medical practice, Ted could want nothing

from the inmates other than for them to behave like medical patients. If they argued, he would repeatedly send them away until they realized that medicine was his game, and there was no way of going around him. Eventually, the prisoners understood that they wanted something from Ted—mainly treatment and medicine— and that he wanted nothing from them. For him, to want anything from them would have put them in charge of him.

In human interaction, the basic fundamental is that our effectiveness is dependent on whether, in the first three years of life, we have established solid, independent identities. Without strong self-images, we are relegated to the poor, second best adaptations of seeking our identities through allegiance with others or joining groups that have been established by others. The great handicap with this secondary adjustment is that we take on the vulnerability of feeling ourselves to be victims. There is no problem with aligning ourselves with groups, as long as we maintain our special identities and totally resist compromising ourselves to the organizations. Instead, we accommodate to the rules as we would in playing table tennis.

If we lack strong self-images, we will

subconsciously perceive our own weakness and, by necessity, seek out stronger persons or godlike images to be our heroes or models. When we dedicate our strong allegiance to powerful groups, we cause ourselves to become their victims. We, as victims, can elicit sympathy and seek solace from gullible or motherly persons, but we can never reach our full creative potentials, which can be realized only if we are distinct and separate persons.

It is universally appreciated that, in counseling, if patients do not and will not relinquish their stances as "victims," there is little that can be done constructively for them or with them. If we feel or profess that we are victims, we assume the problems lie entirely outside ourselves, and *they* hold the solutions, and *they* need to change to suit our needs. Individual therapy, if it is to be effective, must start with the acknowledgement that we should never expect to have other people change directly for our own comfort and benefit. Any force to change people around us is an attack, and their defenses will become more adamant. Therefore, not only is it illogical to attempt to change others to suit us, but it is impossible.

In therapy, we may create safe places for

patients in order to let them consider that they can only benefit when they make adjustments in their attitudes about their self-worth. Once they own up to the reality that they are the only ones who truly need a revised attitude of their self-worth, then they have the opportunity to alter their lives' circumstances. Once they acknowledge that they alone are the problems, then they empower themselves to find solutions to eliminate their former stance as victims.

Indirectly, it is possible to bring about changes in others, but only passively, for it is done by first creating safe places. When other people feel secure enough to shed some defenses, then they may grow emotionally. We have seen this happen. A grandmother who gave up much or her habitual ardent control by anger saw her daughter become much less defensive, which, in turn, allowed her two granddaughters to become less controlled and more assertive. Treating one generation had a trickle down beneficial effect on two younger generations.

Control and domination can only occur when, due to poor self-images, we feel we need approval from others. At that point, we have put them in charge of us. The only cure is to revise and improve our own self-worth. This is a project only we can undertake, and it must start with the acknowledgement that we are creating all aspects of our life experience. Then, we can revisit our formative, childhood, emotional experiences and reinterpret them from our adult perspective to draw new positive conclusions about ourselves and our self-worth.

Anger and Dependence

When we express anger towards others, we are dependent on them, for our "good" depends on their action or inaction. We have automatically declared that we are their victims. The avowed purpose of anger is to get others to act on our behalf or be eliminated for our benefit. On the surface, this behavior would seem to put us in charge, but actually, it is quite the opposite. From the time of our births, our angry cries are evidence that we demand service from others and, thereby, we put others in charge of us. In early infancy, we are totally dependent on our caretakers, and if they are angry with us, we feel rejected, and we feel we may possibly be left to die. As infants, even anger between parents will be registered only as anger toward ourselves, because our subconscious minds attribute all experience to ourselves. In this instance, we perceive that our parents are expecting and demanding that we do something for them. The simple formula is that the caretakers' anger equals rejection, which equals the threat of death.

When we view our dysfunctional society, we can see that a great number of personal interactions are merely reenactments of infantile and childish behaviors. Angry attitudes, with their age-related behavioral traits, are representative of the least emotionally developed individuals and are the most disruptive in interpersonal relationships. The most obvious marker of immaturity and dependence is the readiness with which we can be provoked and goaded into intense displays of anger. Our infant displays of anger can also be regarded as automatic reactions to turn the table on parents and make them victims whose good is dependent on our relaxation and satisfaction.

Obesity and Shame

For the obese among us, dieting is rarely of any long-term help and can even exacerbate our problems. The behavior of obese persons involves a driving need that cannot be satisfied. Seeking gratification through habitual overeating only partially and temporarily satisfies this subconscious drive to fill emptiness, which can, at times, be almost frantic. The acute momentary need to assuage this feeling negates any reflective concern for long term consequences. In the obese, food and eating are the substitutes for fulfilling a deeper drive that is almost as important as life itself. When under stress, obese people eat with determination, as if their lives depend on satiation of that deep survival drive. This urgent consumption of food is in spite of the fact that they are intellectually aware that gross over-weight will shorten their lives and impair their social human interactions. The drive is compelling and immediate, indicating that this behavior depicts a subconscious drive for survival itself. Long-term consequences compared to immediate survival are totally unimportant. This attitude is void of any time frame; it is entirely normal only for infants, whose dependency needs require instant satiation. Obviously, we have an anachronism here; we have a demonstration of an emotional arrest in early infancy. When we examine the logic of this situation, we find that overeating makes no sense at all; therefore, the behavior belongs to another time and place. Analysis of the origin of the basic need for overeating begins with the obvious observation that the drive to overeat is a conversion of a very primal need and is an anachronism in adult behavior. This cannot be the future; it must belong to the past. Also, it is apparent that the instigating stimulus is not low blood sugar, starvation, or endocrine disorder, although, there may be exceedingly rare exceptions to the last. Therefore, the drive must be converted from another imperative; and it is. Second only to the motivation to sustain physical existence is the need for acceptance for being the individuals we are.

The dysfunction arises when we are forced, for our souls' sakes, to assume self-images that deviate from the preordained templates inscribed in our individual genetic codes; that is, we have to compromise our true potentials, which are inscribed in the blueprints of our individual DNA. In early infancy, in order to survive, we are forced to assume personas of the contrived individuals that our caretakers want us to be.

Our vital need, as infants, is to be treated as equal and separate individuals; we are not part of our parents, nor are we their possessions. It is idealistic and romantic to consider that babies will automatically love their mothers. In reality, we, as infants, have no ability or capacity for adult altruistic love, but rather have only survival and dependency needs, including shelter, nurture, warmth, closeness, acceptance, and intuitive communication.

As infants, we communicate with our parents through the seven senses—sight, sound, touch, taste, smell, intuition, and attitude. Intuition and attitude are our primary modes of interactive connection to our mothers, and in a sense, are our first language, comprising the intimate relationships in our first year before our cognitive brains are functioning to any useful degree. Consequently, we depend on our inborn responses to our seven senses to find satisfaction of our vital survival needs. These needs include air, food, water, warmth, and protection in the physical environment, plus our emotional dependency needs. It is vital that we, as infants, have stable, safe places, in which to physically develop, and that, as distinct individuals, we be respected as equals, and therefore be *esteemed* as we are. We are now separate, and, in reality, we have never been parts of our mothers. When both our survival and dependency needs are adequately supplied, we will have the maximum opportunity to evolve into emotionally independent, mature adults.

To insure normal physical development and growth, we need a diet that contains all the proper carbohydrates, fats, proteins, minerals, and vitamins. If specific nutritional deficiencies in minerals occur, such as a shortage of iodine, the endocrine system will not develop normally. Even if we, as infants, secrete enough thyroxin hormone from our thyroid glands, a shortage of iodine in the diet will create cretinism, which results not only in small physical size, but also causes mental retardation. And although, as infants, we may have normal outputs of parathyroid hormone from our parathyroid glands, insufficient intake of calcium will result in rickets. Comparable emotional growth defects will develop when the needed emotional support is lacking at specific times.

At birth and throughout infancy, we must first get *acceptance* of our normal development and *esteem* for our separate individualities from our families, or we cannot sustain acceptance and esteem for ourselves. During our initial two months, and up to two years, we will form our most important attitudes about ourselves— our self-esteem, our self-worth, and our self-placement in the position of relative importance among all others. As these attitudes are formed, they become lifelong directors of our base behavior and will determine how we feel about ourselves concerning our places in human society and our right to be here. Very early in life we are forced to automatically make judgments of our self-worth. We make these decisions long before we are prepared to do so, for we are handicapped by infantile brains that are only partly connected and functioning.

Emotional growth, like physical growth, can be stunted when one or more normal streams of energy are forced to shut down or are diverted. The chief of these inborn emotional streams is the drive to be accepted as we are and esteemed for our potentials as separate individuals. That part of the innate drive that constitutes identity includes the need and freedom to express curiosity, inventiveness, assertiveness, industry, and exploration, as well as the necessity to touch and to be touched, and most of all, the need to be accepted as we are.

If, in the first three years of life, any of these streams are shut down or partially stifled, we are not able to develop our full identities, and instead, we have weak or poor self-images and lack self-esteem. Without strong self-images, our creativity can never be fully realized. To the list of serious personality arrests resulting from emotional crippling in the first three years, including professional homelessness, wife beating, physical violence, drug addiction, and alcoholism, we need to add marked obesity.

These serious behavioral problems represent distortions or blockages (attitudinal bulkheads) formed in infancy for one or more of the streams of emotional energy. Obesity has a more limited area of damage than most of the others. It can be traced to the corrupting of the innate need for closeness and affection. Here is the frequent scenario: A mother may have a severe handicap in that she has little self-esteem and is only partially accepting of herself. Limited by this emotional impairment, she is needy. She covets emotional support from her infant and will do whatever she can to keep her child "loving her." She hopes that by servicing her baby diligently, she will finally get some self-esteem. The mother's unrealistic expectations are profoundly problematic. We cannot earn esteem by doing. And, as infants, we cannot demonstrate adult type love, but are able to communicate only by relaxation when our dependency needs are met.

We might regard this as a case of miscommunication. The infant demands touching, warmth, and acceptance, but expresses these needs only by crying. The mother is limited in her ability to accept anyone, because of her own inadequate self-development, self-esteem, and the lack of self-acceptance. She radiates tension and anxiety. She expresses her adoration for her infant by oversupplying food to placate and buy affection, but the infant is sadly incapable of expressing love in return, although he can and does radiate an attitude of satisfaction when some of his wants and needs are met.

The mother's limited appraisal of her own self-worth restrains her from giving herself fully, with relaxed warmth, to the measure that can be satisfying to the infant's need for security. The child's appetite for food can be satiated much more easily, and this is accomplished long before the fulfilling of his craving for closeness and warmth.

A mother can be very well tuned into her child's need for something. However, if she is hassled, busy, and preoccupied, her ability to intuitively read the infant's subtle need for closeness can well be overlooked. When her child is fussy and crying, it is much easier to prepare large amounts of milk in the bottle than to take relaxed time to warmly hold and intuitively communicate and interact with him.

In this scenario, the infant ingests milk or food until his hunger is satiated but continues to cry because his emotional needs are not met. The mother's remedy is more food. The infant then attempts to satisfy his gnawing need for intimacy and eats until his stomach is overly distended. This is a repeated end point; the child learns that this is the best satisfaction he can get.

This misinterpretation of the infant's emotional

needs and the consequent remedy of oversupply of food reoccur hundreds of times. When the infant perceives that his normal need for closeness, warmth, and understanding is an unwanted trait and is perceived as *an offensive part of his personality,* he reactively submerges and represses it by the formation and adoption of a revised, lesser attitude about himself—that he is flawed and unacceptable. As a reactive consolation, he is taught that he can get approval from his mother by consuming large amounts of food. The only solace for his undesirable need is accepting the partial satisfaction of a distended stomach.

Those of us with this crippling defect often feel small inside. Our basic drive will always be to become those individuals whose potentials are encoded in our DNA, but this drive is blocked and diverted. It is like a grafted apple tree; the rootstock furnishes the energy (sap) to be itself, but the graft bears a foreign fruit. Eating can be controlled for short periods of time, but under strains, especially emotional stress, the feeling generated by a distended stomach can approximate closeness and understanding—an association that will continue subconsciously throughout life, despite all conscious attempts to change.

Overeating is epidemic in America and there are virtually no reliable cures. Widespread understanding of the cause and wide adoption of a new style of child rearing is the hope for the future.

Remedial aid for currently obese persons is available, but it is difficult. We realize that change in repeated behavior can be temporarily helpful, but only the revision of feelings, that is, attitudes about our own identities, will have any lasting effect on our standard behavior. Except for understanding, logic and reason will form no useful part of this therapy. We must gain new information in a form that is in keeping with and non-threatening to the infantile parts of our brains.

There can be another layer of dysfunction, when our caretakers' disregard results in our belief that we must be flawed, and, in turn, we feel shame for being ourselves. We may then want to avoid intimacy because we believe that if anyone truly knew us, they would reject us. Obesity is an ideal way to keep many others from seeking intimacy with us. It is one way to get others to agree with our belief that there is something undesirable about us and so we get the consolation prize of being right.

Permutations of Anger

In general, we act first, or at least we have the urge to act first, and then think later. We, like all living creatures, are designed to sustain life as it is, before we take any new actions or change any established past habits. In microseconds, our subconscious minds will scan our immediate environments, our situations, and all of our sensory inputs for any possible dangers as recognized from past experiences. Successful survival relies on the information that we learned from past experiences and challenges. Unless we make concerted efforts to change our behaviors, our automatic subconscious controls will direct us to repeat those actions that allowed us to live through past similar threats or experiences. Our automatic reenacting, coping defenses are all related to those times in our lives when we first acquired them.

Anger is the primary survival reaction. In the evolution of developing animals, it appears as the first synchronized, operating, reactive device and is only one notch higher in order above the simple spinal cord stimulation-withdrawal reflex. In lower vertebrate animals, this anger response subsides as soon as the initiating stimulus clears. An animal with a slightly more advanced nervous system can hold some individual memory, which will enable the animal to sustain an anger response, thereby maintaining claim to his territory.

The initial crying of a newborn infant is angry and aggressive, a most primitive display for survival. As soon as the infant senses a need or want, he demands attention. The newborn is in trouble if he cannot cry at birth; he needs to get someone to fulfill his survival and dependency needs. This initial cry is indiscriminate, appearing to be the same for all needs, and it is wholly undirected, without any focus toward any particular caretaker.

From birth onward, our developing nervous systems and brains should have an ever-moderating effect as to assigning the cause of discomfort and focusing on the person from whom we demand attention. Consider a three-month-old baby, who perceives that he is deserted because he is unattended; he's in panic, screaming, turning red, and flailing about in rage. This three-month-old has not yet developed enough higher mental management function to moderate or direct his offensive outburst in any way, but has evolved enough to sustain his anger for a prolonged period. Now, imagine this same rage reaction in a twenty-year-old, six-foot-tall man. Would we want to be near him? Would we try to reason with him? If we ask him why he has this attitude, would we expect him to respond or answer any of our questions?

This twenty-year-old man has the attitude of the infantile personality arrest. In essence, he feels as vulnerable as an infant, and therefore, continues this defensive behavior, which expresses an immediate demand for everyone to do something for him. He feels he must fight for his life, without concern for any other person or thing. Accordingly then, when he perceives a threat, he reacts with the primitive, normal, defensive behavior of an infant, which originated from a threat to his survival in infancy.

This raging twenty-year-old has chosen to resist even his slightest urge to act as an adult. To have any command over his situation, he is required to use his higher intellectual brain centers. He accordingly accommodates his insecurity and fear by allowing his primitive brainstem and midbrain to increasingly take over, unchecked. He behaves exactly as he would have done previously, more than nineteen years earlier. However, he is large and physically coordinated, and this renders him infinitely more dangerous.

For an instant, when this fellow first got embroiled in this particular incident of rage, he possessed some moderating capacity to cap his anger, but instead of using it, he choose to make no effort to check his escalating, unbridled emotions. Without any thoughtful attempt to appraise the cause of his rebuff, he gave in totally, allowing his anger to grow as he progressively reverted back emotionally in the reenactment of his infantile behavior. He not only overrode his intellect, but also allowed his anger to recruit all of the hurtful impressions stored in his subconscious mind, thereby encouraging himself to become violent. He retrogressed into an uncontrollable infantile state of blind rage—the state behind the O.J. Simpson murders.

In general, the more infantile personality arrests we have, the more easily we are provoked and the more sustained will be our use and display of anger. Maturing through infancy and beyond, we would normally grow emotionally and then be able to utilize the moderating influence of our developing nervous systems to voluntarily suppress and control unbridled anger. As we physically grow, our nervous systems become progressively connected and functioning. As mammals, our initial endowments are our primitive reptilian brains. We progress to have additional limbic brains, and finally mature to develop our mammalian brains with fully functioning neocortexes. Anger is fueled by the basic survival and aggression imperative emanating from our primordial reptilian brains, which, when combined with fear, can have numerous permutations. Our mammalian brains give us the veto power and ability to moderate and direct our primary offensive forces of aggression, anger, and sex. As we acquire greater mental dexterity, we become capable of adding vivid remembrance of increasing numbers of past alleged traumas. As preventative defenses, we automatically recruit more and more of these active images to create *fears for the future*, which become amalgamated and energized with anger from the past to create a whole list of permutations of anger. Using the offensive drive of anger, in combination with fear, we can generate attitudes which are sustained, antisocial, and self-protective complex emotional responses.

All the permutations of anger and fear have one common purpose, which is to extend and control ourselves, another person, or a situation. In every episode, the angry person behaves as if he himself is the victim. He wants something or some person to do his bidding or change to satisfy his desires and demands. When the permutations of anger are coupled with fear, they further enable that angry person to attempt to control something or someone in the near or distant future. The angry individual or group can be a social annoyance, or, as in war, a lethal threat, by maintaining individual or communal maladapted interpersonal relationships. Psychologically, in consolidating closer interpersonal relationships, the angry person is always a predetermined loser.

Emotionally, he perceives himself to be a victim; therefore, his good inevitably must come from someone else's change for his personal benefit. He starts out with the attitude that some person, thing, or animal "owes him," and he expects and mandates that something be done for him; his expectations are largely unrealistic. This is the absolute cause of anger.

Anger is very personal. It arises in microseconds when we perceive that the integrity of our being is encroached upon by persons, animals, or things. Anger can be induced by threat of death, but threatened physical injury is less of a factor than impending compromise of our separate identities and self-respect. We are driven by this compelling fear of the loss or lessening of identity. Our natural primitive attitude is that the world and all of its creatures should honor and respect our personal status.

At the age of three years and beyond, we should have developed increasing senses of responsibility, but we still can be provoked to anger when others are treating us with their disrespect. However, with increasing maturity, we can manage to moderate or cap the expression of anger. Intellectually, we can understand that the problem lies in the others' perceptions of our individualities. We can never solve other people's problems, since they are rooted in their belief systems.

Because the quality of life is largely controlled by

the number of choices we have, anger is the most limiting and devastating attitude of all. An excellent example is exhibited by whole groups of people in the Middle East who practice and hallow ancient hatreds. When they are actively angry and vengeful, their brains are operating at an infantile intellectual level, making their problems impossible to resolve. When we feel inadequate, we seek to control or destroy whomever we feel are our nemeses. Inevitably, sustained anger turns our bodies' systems against us to cause aging and self-degeneration. Consider an individual with frequent sustained anger—how much exhausting emotional energy does he turn inwardly against himself causing damage and premature aging?

One disclaimer is appropriate. Anger can be life saving because, in microseconds, anger and aggression can marshal all our bodies' systems for defense. We cannot rid ourselves of this primordial ability. With maturity, we can limit its use and the degree of its activity by restricting it to use only to assure our physical and emotional survival. It is an essential backup in extreme emergencies where there is dire need for instant activation of the total body resources. Even this activation should be for only a limited time, because, after a short time, a person's actions must be moderated advantageously as he allows his higher mental centers to be used to further extricate himself from extreme danger. A temporary show of anger can be helpful to maintain our territory—for instance when somebody is approaching us for sexual favors, uninvited. Anger, like the flu, can be contagious, and whereas anger at a social injustice can be helpful in promoting a crusade with a cause, much more commonly, anger excites a brawl or a mob or a war. Anger is like a hot coal which is hard to handle, but can be used to self-motivate and overcome our own misconduct or ineptness. Anger can act as a motivation to push us to prove our points or to accelerate achievements. It can act as a spur for determination, goal setting, and other productive endeavors.

With maturity, we have an increasing ability to suppress or moderate our expression of both our sex drive and the use of anger. In addition, when anger wells up, we can choose to let it subside without physical action, express it mildly, or let it have free reign. The more we let it grow, the baser it becomes, until, in extreme cases, its expression can culminate in blind, mindless, killing rages.

With cognitive thought, we can intensify our anger by recalling related incidents from the past. To get all the permutations of anger, we can combine anger with fear of the future. The standard combination of anger plus fear forms predictable syndromes, which cause a multitude of disagreeable attitudes. These combinations of anger and fear become more subtle and complicated as we enlarge our perceptions during the developmental ages of one to six years. These permutations of anger are expressed as attitudes, which are all age-related. They are common and standard enough so that people with similar personality arrests can join together with a common cause, for example, in hate groups.

Further Permutations of Anger

During infancy, or birth to three years, our neocortexes have no significant ability to form calculated appraisals. In other words, we lack perspective. The reptilian segments of our nervous systems can and do mainly keep us in running order; they exhibit behaviors of undirected anger as a survival technique. Late in infancy, the limbic portions of our brains become increasingly organized in the ability to form images and defenses.

Some infantile permutations of anger are fussiness (6 months to 2 ½ years), crankiness (1 to 2 years), tantrums (3 months to 2 years), and sullenness (2 to 3 years). Childhood permutations of anger include hate, bigotry, bullying, temper, and temper tantrums.

The temper tantrum is a reactive expression in which the individual has the feeling that he has no effect whatsoever on his surroundings. This personality arrest is exemplified by the classic presentation of a three-month-old baby lying on his back, unable to turn over, kicking, screaming, and turning red. In later months or years, the same attitude of utter ineffectiveness is expressed as frustration and a reenactment of this three-month-old behavior. In teenage years, this same sense of ineffectiveness and ineptness can be expressed by engaging in youthful vandalism or juvenile delinquency. Here, the anger is acted out with typical, infantile, total disregard of not only others and their rights, but also of the individual's own future good.

To every question and suggestion, a normal two-year-old's typical first response is, "No." This response is an essential part of his declaring himself to be a separate individual. When he perceives himself to be unduly pressured, he may respond in anger. When we add the anger or aggression to the normal intransigence of a two-year-old, we get rebellion. Rebellion blocks any peaceful resolution, for the two-year-old is defending himself for the sake of his individual integrity. His body is so designed that defense, once initiated, will cut off the use of any higher cognitive selections to moderate his behavior. When the two-year-old becomes more adamant in going his own way, he becomes aggressive. Aggressiveness, at any age, is an offensive action; the individual is mindless of others' feelings and rights. This rebellion is an emotional arrest characterized by age-reenactment of behavior that belongs to an earlier, most primitive state.

When a two-year-old perceives that he is totally thwarted in his assertiveness, he may respond by demonstrating unbridled anger, that is, defiance. A youngster in this state of anger, unmindful of fear, becomes unconcerned with any consequence of this behavior.

When a three-year-old child is taught, by repeated example, to be fearful of any group of people, places, or things, this familial attitude of prejudice is a pervasive teaching. He will adopt this attitude as naturally as he will adopt his parents' language and regional accent. Our families' attitudes constantly remind us that we are part of them; therefore we, too, have been victimized by those people, places, and situations. Our caretakers transfer their virus of anger-combined-with-fear into a self-perpetuating mindset of hate, which is a double no-brainer for it shuts off intellectual thought with both anger and fear defenses.

A four-year-old can demonstrate slow burning anger by becoming reluctant and perverse and by displaying anger as passive aggression. At age four, when we find that our views or actions are ignored and rebuffed, we feel completely blocked. When we fear the future, we persist in continuing what we know to be safe, and then, as a consequence, we create stubbornness. Frustration occurs when, in a semi-passive way, we suppress and convert our energy into slow-burning anger, which we repeatedly display as resentment and bitterness. In a more subtle display, we can show some of our anger in the use of sarcasm.

In today's society, the most acceptable and frequently used form of anger is argumentation—a four-year-old personality arrest. Rather than making a declamatory statement or seeking a meaningful discussion, we make an authoritative pronouncement, perhaps using anger for emphasis, designed to achieve avoidance of any clarifying questions. In taking this approach, we are acting defensively. That is, when threatened, rather than explaining our views, we feel the necessity to defend and force our beliefs and prejudices upon our alleged adversaries and enemies.

The argumentative attitude is that if others reject our points of view, they reject us as persons; therefore, we must defend ourselves, for our lives' sake. In argumentation, the instant that we start defending ourselves, anger will preclude our own higher thought centers from any possible deliberation in finding solutions to common problems or variances in personal beliefs.

The instant that we employ any degree of any form of anger, we enter "no-brain" defensive struggles for power. If others argue back, then we are all in a no-brain melee in which nothing useful can be learned or resolved. No new ideas are exchanged, but rather, we are in search of ammunition to attack our enemies in power struggles. The object of these power struggles is to inflict our dogma on others.

A five-year-old dictator has learned that if he adds anger to his voice when he makes a statement, he may convey that he is the authority. That is, he implies that what he states is fact, thereby defying any questioning or hint that what he has just pronounced is anything but the absolute final word. In addition, any command given in anger is done with the hope of subjugating all others and preventing any non-compliance. This intimidation, when it takes a physical form, is known as bullying.

The general principle restated is: The guiding drive either for or against an activity will be determined by the related impressions we have acquired and stored in our subconscious minds. Whether we are for or against, we are ruled by a single principle—whether we are fearful and yield meekly to power and oppression or use coercive power because we perceive ourselves to be impotent, we have kept the concept of power as our driving directional force.

Bigotry has a formulation very similar to that of hate, but recruits more fear and less anger. At a five-year-old level, when our brains are more organized in the formulation of thoughts, we have the ability to concoct visions and schemes for revenge. We start out with a basic slow burn of residual anger, and on this, we superimpose the feelings stimulated by revived images of past alleged victimization. Then, as we add collected fears, we supercharge this proactive defense as revenge. Revenge compels us, with this drive for self-protection, to destroy the alleged offending persons or things "before they get us."

Temper is a chronic state of mind in which there is a perpetual attitude of underlying anger, causing a constant drain on emotional energy. This underlying infantile attitude includes the perception of being victimized, as in the feeling that we have been wronged when we are not allowed to have our own way. In all displays of temper, our thinking minds have already been disengaged, so that no amount of logic or reasoning will be admitted. With temper, we express anger, always for an alleged personal incursion of the past, in a sustained state of expectation, in which we attempt to right the past by controlling the present.

Irritability is akin to temper, but differs in its focus. We exhibit our tempers when someone else is not fulfilling our expectations in doing things for us. We express irritability when other people do not acknowledge our individualities and make no effort to acknowledge our personhood. Irritability is a self-sustained, low-grade angry state of mind in which we feel that we have been slighted and are sort of waiting for something to happen upon which to focus our wrath. Both temper and irritability are often misplaced and centered on those whom we consider lower in our pecking order.

We need to be aware of our justification for our own claim of rightful anger, which can signal that we have a problem. If we live in a totalitarian community or religious state, anger and revenge may be considered to be holy. Even there, however, it is ruinous to interpersonal relationships and intimacy. As we have mentioned, there are a few occasions, in adulthood, when anger is temporarily life saving or helpful. Notably, such an occasion is the sudden occurrence of a cataclysmic event, when, in microseconds, we need maximum stimulation and coordination of all our body's systems to save our lives. In very real terms, when we are faced with mortal combat or simply breaking through our extreme timidity, the use of anger prevents us from being overtaken by paralyzing fear. Also, socially, there is a small place for our anger or angry indignation; our show of anger can stimulate others to support us in championing a worthy cause to right a social injustice. A few people find that becoming angry with themselves prods and motivates them into action. Ultimately, there are very few situations where displays of anger will be the most expedient way for us to stake out our turf.

Anger Summary

Anger and aggression, rather than being defenses, are our primary offensive forces to subjugate, destroy, or kill whatever or whomever we perceive to be threatening. The more vulnerable we feel, the more we need to resort to the use of anger. It is rooted in the reptilian part of our nervous systems, where since ancient times, it has served as the lifesaving force and cannot be removed. It is absolutely essential when we need every system in our bodies to activate quickly to sustain our lives. Anger is so primitive that, when activated, it precludes fear. It can be useful to maintain our territory and occasionally be helpful in motivating ourselves or a group to champion a cause. Anger has little useful place in adult behavior and almost always chills or destroys good interpersonal relationships. The expression of anger usually represents an infantile demand for respect for individuality and personhood. It is used extensively by individuals who feel that they are victims. The anger and aggression drive can be amalgamated with fear to cause such syndromes as hate, bigotry, and revenge.

The Anger Game

Probably man's oldest game, which is universally played by most families today, is, "Guess and Do." This is the fruitless attempt to appease a family member and prevent an angry outburst. The object of this cruel game is to try to figure out in advance what one must do or say in order to prevent Mommy or Daddy from becoming angry, and thereby, avert the threat of rejection (death). The rules are constantly changing; actions that seemed to formerly placate them now only infuriate them. It is a game where no one wins, and there is no chance that our participation will draw us emotionally closer to our parents or siblings. The most aggressive play includes the feature that, because of our contrariness, our parents have already damaged us.

Grudges and rejections are recorded subconsciously for a lifetime. Amnesty is not part of this game.

As adults, we may still be playing this guessing game, not only with our children, but also with our aging parents. How can this conundrum be solved? Understanding the answer and explanation is simple and straightforward, but the changes necessary to end the game are profound. The problem is based completely on attitudes. That is, we've always started with the premise that there's something wrong with us and that we are directly responsible for our parents' feelings. The reality is that every one of us is solely responsible for our own feelings; we cannot make it right for others. It is the very nature of creation—we cannot solve or cure any other person's emotional problems. True, we can "push their buttons," but in the final count, they are responsible for establishing and maintaining these public conveniences. Secondarily, our attitudes have always been that our traits or behaviors have caused our parents' emotions; we subconsciously believe that we are their problem. From the very start, the primary problem has been our parents, because they are the ones who have the attitude problems—their expectations.

Consider the basic fact of life that we cannot guess or solve another individual's personal emotional problem. For emphasis, in recent years, have we truly solved any personal problems other than our own? When friends have come to us for advice, has our counsel alone changed anything? The most we can hope for is their acceptance of our suggestion that they alone have the opportunity to let a change take place in their attitudes, which will allow solutions to work. Factually, the only other possibility is that we could change to suit their expectations; but we would have to know what their expectations were, and precisely which changes might be acceptable.

The dastardly part of the anger game is that in the first year of our lives, we are recruited to play in deadly earnest. Our assignment is to appease our parents and prevent their anticipated angry outbursts. We are forced to start the interplay when we are merely infants, and, at that time, we don't have enough of our brains organized to comprehend that we are not the center or the cause of every activity about us. Our parents' problem was then, and continues to be, that they have unrealistic expectations of us.

How much of the time have we truly anticipated

the ever changing expectations of our parents, and further, how often have we been right in out-guessing them? If we have trouble now, consider how it must have been when we were only one year old, when our thinking brains and deductive reasoning minds were yet to come online; in normal evolution, these changes come two years later. Even now, we tenaciously cling to the attitude of being at fault that we felt forced to adopt then. Also, our parents persist in maintaining their attitudes and expectations that we, as their infants, are parts of them and should "shape-up" to their personally idealized images and performance standards. Their preconceived pictures were of babies who would match their assigned specifications. Their attitudes were expressed by their expectations of us, and because we did not fit, we have always been at least partial failures.

This discussion is not to be construed as a blatant condemnation singling out our parents. This has been the continuing and sustained familial behavioral custom for generations. Our families and tribal heritages serve us as models for dealing with our own children. Our purpose is to foster an understanding of the dynamic of anger, so that parents can better manage the formation of attitudes in future generations.

Understanding Classroom Gunfire

At any given moment, our memories of past experiences, coupled with our expectations, will determine our behavior. If an event is not emotionally charged, our actions will be more consciously selected, thus giving us greater freedom of choice. If a situation stirs up our emotions especially intensely, particularly in a threatening way, then our behavior will be increasingly automatic and directed by our subconscious minds, corresponding to the magnitude of the perceived threats. Simply put, when emotion goes up, intelligence goes down. The more the occasion strains us, the more our behavior will automatically be determined by scripted defenses which are already in our minds and bodies. These automatic, orchestrated reactions have been developed as responses to an accumulation of past similar experiences. They protect us from experiencing reenactments of the consequences of dreaded, past occurrences.

When, in the first two years of life, we experience a deeply ingrained sense of failure to gain a feeling of acceptance of self and acceptance by others; we can have consuming feelings of aloneness and victimization. When we lack connections with our families and other groups, we feel lost and alone. Some experts suggest that when strong connections are developed with families, schools, etc., such incidences as schoolroom shootings would not occur. This premise sounds entirely reasonable in an orderly society. Going one step deeper, we will find the base cause of lack of connectedness is the failure of individuals to ever have known emotionally safe places. In early infancy, personal safe places should have been established by the infants' caretakers by according the children acceptance as separate and equal individuals—the most important need and drive in humans.

Equal to the drive to stay physically alive is the emotional need for acceptance. An infant needs a safe place to develop according to the template encoded in his individual DNA; that is, he needs to be accepted for the special individual that he is. He achieves connectedness with his family only when he is regarded as a separate and equal individual. If his parents treat him as an object or possession, which simply needs to be trained, he will be dependent upon them for survival, but he will never establish the connection of a close interpersonal relationship with them. If the caretakers override the infant's natural, inborn, behavioral traits and impose performance and suppression commands to shape him up merely to satisfy their conception of what a child should be and do, then this infant has only a dependent, strained, and hostile connection to his parents, while remaining utterly dependent upon them for physical subsistence. In his first year, this emotionally rejected infant establishes a seething anger and resentment that can last a lifetime. Only at a later, safer time, when he is no longer physically dependent upon them, may he vent his hostility on them, or more commonly, transfer it to anyone whom he considers to be treating him as his caretakers did in his infancy. Latent, deep, unabated anger can be regarded as the manifestation of failure to achieve fulfillment of his inborn potential to be a separate and accepted individual, who required a safe place and the support to emotionally become that potential person preordained by his genetic template.

At all times, we do only what we want to do. We can make all kinds of explanations and excuses, but when we get down to the base motivation, the actions we take are what we want. The problem in understanding is that the importance of our subconscious wants, needs, and drive to survive far exceeds what our wishful conscious minds try to elect. No matter how untoward or seemingly inappropriate, the replaying of patterns that successfully saved our lives in the past will prevail. Through the years, our continuous replaying of our infantile or childish behaviors has served the purpose—to keep us alive for the current moment. The factual basis is that untoward behavior, which is entirely out of place for us as adults, would be normal, or at least would be acceptable, if chronologically, we were still infants or children.

To discover the logic of current behavior, we have to totally disregard the chronological age of the reacting person, and, instead, understand subconscious imperatives. That is, we need to age-relate specific attitudes as anachronisms, and only then will the behavior be in its appropriate frame of reference. In the proper age bracket, the attitude or behavior will make logical sense. Specific attitudes and their attendant behaviors are the learned responses to fears, not of adults or teenagers, but of infants or children.

We can analyze the behavior of the teenager shooting and killing his fellow students. Certainly, murder is not normal teenage or adult behavior, or even normal childish behavior, even for a three-year-old. A thirty-six-month-old child with standard emotional maturity has begun to have a strong sense of responsibility. Attitude plus election determines and drives a person's behavior. To understand motive, the salient fact is pegging the age of the attitude of the schoolroom killer. Totally irresponsible gunfire is such a ruthless attitude with its total disregard, not only for other people, but for the individual perpetrator as well, (although only momentarily), that such behavior can only be infantile in origin. We do not ordinary think of infants as killers, but they would be if they were able. For example, consider a three-month-old infant who senses that he is abandoned. He starts with a cry in fear and anger. If still unattended, he intensifies and escalates the anger into rage. Accompanying this rage, he flails his arms and legs out in every possible direction—normal behavior for a three-month-old baby. When a fourteen-year-old makes no attempts to modify or control his anger, but instead, elects to let it go unchecked into a natural, uncontrolled, downward course, he soon reaches the non-contemplative, infantile level of a three-month-old infant. Furthermore, when his anger is intensified with childish, three-year-old level fantasy—his own imagery of continuing persecution—the teenager becomes agitated. View again this raging three-month-old infant, but see him now in the body of fourteen-year-old, physically well developed, coordinated, skilled individual, weighing 140 pounds. Do we try to reason with him or just try to keep out of his range?

If a small infant had a very severe infection, such as meningitis, but survived to become an adult, he could have serious mental and emotional problems that might make it hard for him to adjust to normal society. In a somewhat similar manner, an infant could have a severe emotional assault that would shut off a part of the stream of his emotional maturity. He might continue to grow physically and intellectually, but the assault could have left him stunted in certain areas of emotional development.

An infant is born with all the proper wiring in his head, but his central nervous system does not have all of his synaptic neuron connections hooked up. Consequently, the brain has only very rudimentary emotional control. If he encounters severe emotional assault or deprivation in his emotional evolution, he may become arrested at the age when this occurs. When the teenager is under sufficient situational stress, this emotional arrest in the early months of life will serve as his base level of attitude and his behavior will revert all the way back to this infantile rage. During an easygoing life, this emotionally challenged person can keep the lid on his underlying feelings, but periodically, he may display his short fuse. The more he feels inadequate, left out, ridiculed, and picked-upon, the more he revisits that part of his infancy in which he failed to gain the status of an equal individual and was excluded from the connectedness of family membership. This attitude of emotional deprivation is a public access button, which can be pushed easily to provoke him into displaying infantile anger whenever things go wrong.

Modifying current behavior and learning to cope

can keep the lid on the frequency of outbreaks, but only basic alteration in the teenager's perception of his distorted infantile feelings of self-worth will permanently change his life. That is, whenever he feels inadequate or fails to get respect, he is potentially dangerous.

Our teenager has grown both physically and intellectually, but deep inside, he still has this infantile rage. Initially, his anger is just general, unfocused, and unsustained, because it is solely related to an immediate past event. As he grows older, he modifies and adds three new dimensions to his anger. He learns to focus on his supposed oppressor. He learns to sustain anger by concentrating energy spawned from the imagery that he forms in his head, in which he dwells upon how he has allegedly been wronged. Finally, he combines and compounds anger with fear. This compound of anger and fear can be exhibited as hate and seething in the seeking of revenge. All of this emotional conglomerate can remain smoldering and suppressed, as long as he is not overly stressed. Eventually, his dwelling on and intensifying the images in his head excites his fear, which in turn motivates him to eliminate his supposed oppressors.

We all pretend, at least in some degree, to be

adults and attempt to exhibit acceptable behavior according to the groups with which we associate. However, this pretense is diminished, or is completely gone, when we are under stress, especially if it is sudden or unanticipated. When we "put our best foot forward," we are acting out our self-portraits, because we are attempting to behave as we would like others to see us. However, when under increasing strain, we may no longer be able to suppress our underlying drives. Consequently, we act out our defense programs. At this point, our behavior becomes semiautomatic and we simply direct it. We display those learned and rehearsed scenarios recorded in our defense systems. This behavior is controlled by our attitudes, our beliefs about ourselves and how we relate to others or how they are threatening to us. The element of choice in that moment is that we pick the target, but the stream of emotion is automatic.

The most useful way to view dysfunctional society is to classify each attitudinal dysfunction by its appropriate age, that is, infant or child. In the best of times, we act out in accordance with the self-contrived pictures of the persons we wish ourselves to be, that is, our self-portraits. Maintaining this fantasy creates a constant strain, for it is an act and does not coincide with how we truly feel ourselves to be. Under stress, even in spite of added effort to prevent detection, we repeatedly display slight or major breaks that cause us to behave in ways that are inconsistent with our self-portraits. The most common of these is inaccurate speech. For example, we often hear people say, "I could care less," by which they intend to mean, "I don't care." In fact, the phrase they say actually reveals that they do care. Only if you really care about something could you ever consider caring less.

As we analyze our schoolboys and their shooting of their teacher and classmates, we can break down the components of their behavior. First, the errant students behaved with total disregard for the future of the other people, or even themselves. They behaved with reckless abandon, doing only what they wanted to do, which is normal behavior only for infants. Next, they attempted to eliminate or destroy whatever they identified as "unconnected" to them and as irritating. This behavior represents the venting of their pent-up anger compounded by fear in the form of revenge, which is the ultimate in assigning feelings.

Anger is a primitive force that it is found even in

lower life forms. When we are experiencing the first few milliseconds of anger, and we make no attempt to stop its expression, but rather choose to lose all control, anger becomes so fundamentally primitive that it bypasses any higher intellectual considerations. When anger is totally unsuppressed by choice, it reverts back to infantile rage, striking out in all directions in an offensive effort to gain respect, control, and fulfillment of desires.

The schoolboys' anger was not an immediate response, but a delayed and calculated act, which requires additional components. This delay indicates a higher evolutionary order, for a true infant will tolerate no delay. The anger is the undergirding, and when it is compounded with more sophisticated, focused fear, it creates direction, which requires reasoning more complex than that of an infant. With the increased brainpower of a three-year-old, we learn to focus and identify the person who is pushing us around. With this ability to direct thought, we can form resentment—the residual form of seething anger. Yet, there is an additional component—that of a five-year-old who has been taught revenge, a concept which is blatantly sanctified and even glorified in our culture.

In addition, in our society, movies and television glamorize heroes, who are granted unrestrained license to "get even." The violence of hours of television demonstrates repeatedly the approved method of how to proceed when other people oppress us or get in our way. Teens may also have spent countless hours playing video games, gaining great skill in hand-eye coordination, shooting, and blowing things up. All of this "entertainment" is void of emotion, except for excitement and a sense of accomplishment. Far too seldom, on TV and in the movies, do creators ever show the hero having bad consequences for his inhumane or unlawful acts. As we gain skill in destruction and killing in our video games, we develop macho images, free of remorse and compassion.

The feelings that induced this triad of personality arrests are those of an individual who feels trapped in a situation in which he is a powerless victim. There is nothing that he can do or say that has any effect on correcting or adjusting "those people" around him who run the world.

As infants, we need every support for our own ideas, actions, and initiative. However, because our caretakers know that they are bigger, stronger, and wiser, they think they must constantly be in control. Consequently, we, as infants, are interrupted in our natural flow of exploration, investigation, and experimentation, because we are being corrected and directed in all our actions. From infancy, we, by treatment and example, are made to feel that we do not belong and are inadequate. Our caretakers, by their personal behavior, demonstrate that we deserve no family connections. After all, we are just possessions; "My children." When this feeling of separation is part of our self-images, achieving later multiple successes does not automatically change our feelings of inadequacy.

Each time we impose commands on an infant that interfere with his learning, we build hesitation, doubt, and anger. The infant's chief protection for the retention of any his self-respect is anger. An angry outburst is meant to counteract outside control, in an attempt to wrestle back domination. If this process of protective isolation is intense, continues for long periods, and is often repeated, the infant, out of necessity, will develop a personality arrest of anger, which will serve him the rest of his life. When he feels totally ineffective, he may display anger, which is the automatic weapon to get respect from the people around him. Of course, as a teenager or an adult, this attempted manipulation will never be fulfilling. He truly wants, not respect, but acceptance and esteem for who he is. Even here, the ultimate is not acceptance by others, but rather his acceptance of himself.

In summary, random shooting and killing is an infantile act of rage. In a sense, it is the normal extension of anger of a three-month-old flailing his arms and legs out in every direction in a primitive attempt to eliminate, destroy, or kill whatever or whomever he feels is oppressing him or denying him his individuality. For the teenager, this basic drive for survival is slightly different, because his intellect has matured, making it possible to direct his added fear, compounded with anger, to permit the sophisticated planning to get revenge. This revenge is premeditated. He plots and focuses his energy to eliminate any or all of those whom he perceives as the oppressors who, when he was an infant, treated him as a "nothing."

Truth and Reality

Emotionally speaking, reality can be very simply defined as honesty with ourselves. Demanding respect from others, but not giving any esteem to ourselves, is self-delusion. "Doing our own things" has no relationship to "being our own persons." It is important to understand the difference between being and doing. We get acceptance for who we are; we seek approval for what we do.

There are two levels of trust—trusting others, and trusting ourselves for being ourselves. They both involve insight and the application of awareness to the limit and extent to which we can confidently apply this information. We may hear the old maxim, "I don't care about history. I'm only interested in the present." It is our observation and experience that, when making reasonable assumptions about a person's future, the history of his past behavior under stress is a reliable measure. When trying to make a prediction about what another person will do, how he will react, or what he will become, our most reliable information is found by studying his past actions and reactions. In evaluating the amount of faith that we should invest in predicting another person's future behavior, we need to recall and use all of our observations of his past behavior.

When using this mental exercise, we rely on some information more than other. We weight about 75% of our estimates on the history of past behavior when under emotional stress, and then determine the remaining 25% by our current perceptions, guided by our gut feelings. We intuitively evaluate attitude, that is, the way in which the other person emotionally makes his statements. Words mean very little compared to nuances that we glean from listening and observing the manner in which the other person tells his tale. The obvious problem is that we are never able to know the full, detailed history of another person's past behavior. In general, people under stress are amazingly true to form year after year, so often, gaining snippets of their history is highly revealing when combined with listening and observing skillfully. The summation of all of this information gives us up to 90% accuracy in our ability to predict the future behavior of others.

As for trusting ourselves, there is an enormous historical truth bound up in our subconscious minds, where we have a 100% record of our own experiences and past behaviors when under pressure. Theoretically, we should be able to trust ourselves 100% of the time and this trust is a true reality for the emotionally evolved individual.

We come into this world with expectations for survival, because our instincts are programmed for the continuation of the species; therefore, we are entirely self-centered. Early in infancy, we adopt our lifelong attitudes about our self-worth, which become semi-permanently engraved in our subconscious minds when under emotional stress. Shortly after birth, our caretakers force us to adopt adjusted attitudes of our self-worth. These adjusted attitudes are compromises, which demand less than complete self-acceptance. We are inoculated with alien beliefs outside our personal DNA, like viruses, which are transmitted by absorption from exposure to our parents.

Similarly, we assume our caretakers' values of respect or disrespect for one another. When there is little or no acceptance of one parent for the other or for themselves individually, then we acquire this same feeling of lack of worthiness. As a consequence of making adjustments to our environments, we have to compromise our separate individualities, our souls. Simply to keep our bodies alive through the period of infancy and childhood, we reactively renounce those traits that are demonstrated, by our parents' anger, to be unwanted.

As adults, we can appreciate the distinction between compromise and accommodation. When, as infants, we have to adopt some of our caretakers' attitudes for our lives' sake, we are forced to compromise by forfeiting some integrity. During those first years, we cannot evaluate the effect of surrendering those parts of our souls. When we go against the developmental programs encoded in our genes, we stir up, within ourselves, uncomfortable intuitive signals. These signals are generated from the contest between what we know instinctively is right for us, and what we are forced to do or believe in order to placate our caretakers. Our intuitive understanding is swept away, which enables us to adopt the dictates and to forcefully act out behaviors that are poor counterfeits of our true self-images. These displays of "flawed self" are the pretenses that our parents want to see. The portrayals are those of children modeled after themselves or what they considered to be their "wanted child."   Our caretakers indicate that their formulation is the only way in which we should regard ourselves.

As adults, in order to be successful in marriages and community relations, we are required to accommodate many silly customs, rules of conduct, and laws prescribed by others. These acknowledgments and adjustments can be nuisances, but do not comprise or denigrate our basic beliefs about ourselves. As children, however, we cannot argue or defend ourselves against silly procedures and policies, even though, when they are imposed upon us, they cause us to lose self-worth. Nevertheless, we have to swallow them. Today, we continue to subconsciously obey the same sense of diminished self, as these imposed attitudes continue to rule. Any attempted deviation from this repeating command performance that our parents wanted will cause a frightening feeling of discomforting shame. Not pleasing our parents, even forty years later, is alarming.

Our subconscious minds remember and reexperience the same threat of losing our lives as they experienced it many years ago. Here is the tremendously hurtful rule by which we have always lived: "My learned, initial, infantile, or childish behavior got me by to live another day and continues to do so today." We are still alive; therefore these defense responses must be continuing to work for us.

Our automatic, lifesaving defenses will not let us consider any alteration of this learned and practiced behavior. Although we are no longer infants or children, and have consequently ceased needing these defenses, the task to revamp the subconscious rules by which we have always lived can be accomplished only by adjustment of our attitudes about ourselves. Any revision of a belief can be done only by enlargement of the body of accurate information upon which our beliefs are initially founded.

Enlarging the area of discovery about ourselves will alter our beliefs, which in turn, will change automatically with the revision of our attitudes. New attitudes about our self-images will result in upgraded, more mature behavior.

Management of Feelings

When we have strong, overpowering emotions such as anger, grief, or fear, which intrude upon our awareness and cannot be dismissed, then we have a choice as to how to manage these feelings. The conventional choice, and the one which enjoys cultural support, is to assign the feelings to the situation in which they occur. For example, if we are driving on the freeway and someone rudely cuts us off, we may, if we are so inclined, feel anger. If we feel anger, we have a choice. We can think to ourselves, "That idiot! That inconsiderate, ill-mannered, aggressive fool! I'd like to run him off the road or pull him out of his car and punch him out." In doing so, we have assigned our anger to his actions. In other words, we say to ourselves, "I'm feeling this because he did that." This is a position that has wide acceptance in our society, especially in relationships. If our significant others say critical things or inconvenience us, and we feel upset, either hurt or angry, we may accost them and say, "Why did you say that? That really upset me!" and the argument can proceed from there. The phrasing assigns our feelings to the event or to another person's speech. So, in these cases, we are saying that the circumstances from which our emotions arise are the causes of the emotions.

What's the problem with this? The main problem is that it is not reality-based; in reality, we supply the emotion to absolutely everything that happens in our lives. There is nothing in our lives that absolutely demands that one emotion or another be experienced. For example, if we're walking down the street and somebody runs up, glares at us, and stomps on our feet, we may feel fearful or angry, and we may attribute our emotions to the event. In other words, we think, "That man looked threateningly at me, stomped on my foot, and that hurt, so of course, I'm angry," or, "Of course, I'm fearful."

However, suppose that just before we walk down the street, we run into a billionaire who says, "You know,

I'm a sporting man, and my friend and I here have a little wager going, and I'll inform you and compensate you for your role in it. Our wager is that I think this is a safe street and that nothing bad ever happens to anybody on this street at this time of day. My friend disagrees. I have a large bet with him, and I'll also give you a million dollars if anything unfortunate should happen in your next 20 minutes on this street." So, with this unusual preface, we take our walk down the street as before, and the same event happens–a man runs up, glares at us, stomps on our feet, and leaves. What's our reaction this time? Our reaction is jubilation! We're elated! We throw our hands in the air and say, "Yes!" because the very same experience we did not enjoy previously now makes us rich.

This imagined example is overdrawn to make a point, but the point is valid in all cases, which is: it's not what happens or what is said to us that determines our emotions. Because of embedded expectations, we determine exactly how we are gong to respond based on our prior beliefs and positions. That means we are 100% responsible for all of our emotional responses, since there is no one particular emotion that will be predictably elicited by the same event from all people.

With our ingrained expectations, we are deciding for ourselves, usually pre-deciding for ourselves, which emotions we will have in response to which events. So, assigning our feelings to the speech and behaviors of others, or to the circumstances around us, is not based in reality. That is the biggest problem with the cultural norm of assigning our feelings to the circumstances in which they arise.

So what's the alternative? The alternative is to own all of our feelings as our own. Let's return to our example on the freeway—we're cut off rudely by another driver, who may even flip us the finger. When we feel the anger come up, we can, if we are astute and reality-based, decide to behave within ourselves in ways that are useful to us. That is, we can experience the feelings of anger and separate them from the event. Disregarding the event, we feel the anger in our bodies, usually someplace in the middle of our abdomens, or perhaps in the chest and in our muscles, and we feel this feeling of anger knowing that it is ourselves that we are feeling. In other words, it is our emotion emanating from us—not imposed on us, but generated from within us—which we are feeling.

If we let ourselves feel the anger completely,

accept it entirely, feel it as intensely as it will let itself be felt, we'll notice that true, intense, pure emotions are very brief, lasting only seconds, maybe 15 seconds, at most. The pure experience of emotion can be only briefly sustained. Very soon, after a few seconds, we find ourselves thinking about other things. But for those seconds, we let ourselves totally own and feel the emotion in our bodies. When we do this—when we own emotion—it has the interesting effect of lessening the intensity of the feeling, both at the moment and in the future. It's like the emotion is a bathtub full of water and if we assign emotion or blame to someone or some situation for our feelings, we're just swirling the bathwater around. In fact, people who blame circumstances and other people for their feelings may sustain the insulting image and may think about a past slight or assault for 10 or 20 years and get angry every time it comes to mind. In other words, no progress is ever made in our emotional lives by assigning emotions. However, if we own our emotions and feel them intensely in our bodies as our own, not related to the circumstances in which they arise, then those feelings diminish permanently.

It's like dipping out a teaspoonful of water from a

full bathtub. It may not seem like much, and it may take thousands of repetitions, but in the end the bathtub is drained. So, if we have overpowering emotions based on beliefs, owning those emotions as they occur moment to moment diminishes them, and gradually they become less influential. They come up less powerfully and affect us less and less with each exposure, until eventually, we become large enough and they become small enough that they no longer hold us in their grip. Also, at that point, our underlying belief changes.

This doesn't mean that we can't become angry, only that the anger then seems small, and we recognize it as an old friend. We put our arms around it and draw it close to us and own it, and it actually becomes a neutral sensation rather than something that dominates our awareness and disrupts our senses of well-being. The reality-based approach to emotion is that we increasingly give up the insulting image and own our feelings completely, since they are ours to start with. To assign them is not reality-based; it only perpetuates overpowering emotions, which disrupt our senses of well-being and harmony.

The reality of emotions, as we see, is that circumstances do not cause emotions. Now, as a corollary, what is seldom understood is that just the opposite is true–that emotions cause circumstances. If we are having trouble owning our emotions, nature will help us by making them easier to feel. In other words, the destiny of all human beings is to be whole–not perfect–but whole. A perfect life would include only the things that we define as good–joy, love, wealth, happiness and so on–and none of the things which we label as unpleasant–fear, anger, loss, sadness, poverty, frustration, etc. The truth is that no one has a life composed only of things which he has judged to be desirable. Life is always some of what we like and some of what we don't like. The most a human being can be is whole, meaning that we unrestrictedly open ourselves to experiencing, owning, and loving our lives each moment as they happen. This includes both the things about which we have a favorable judgment and the things we have judged unfavorably.

Now, if we have unexpressed anger, for example, that anger can either be owned in small bits as they come up in our daily lives, or, if we continue to assign it and not own it or include it into our bodies, then nature seems to say "All right, let's make it easier to feel." Then circumstances will arise in our lives that call for ever-increasing levels of anger. They could be small and inconsequential things, like fender bender car accidents, or catastrophic tidal waves, such as personal assaults or other forms of violence.

The tendency of life to move toward wholeness is the driving force for this phenomenon—that our emotions cause our circumstances. The mechanism by which this happens includes the phenomenon that we mentioned earlier—that our perceptions are determined by our beliefs. Consequently, if we are angry, that anger will always be directed at ourselves, since our unconscious minds attribute all thought content to themselves. Now, if we are extremely angry at others, we tend to do things that are likely to hurt them. We put them in dangerous positions, cause them to make choices that could involve harm, and induce them to say things that incite conflict. This is exactly what we do with ourselves. If we are angry, our anger will automatically be directed at ourselves. It's impossible to be angry at others without having that same anger apply to ourselves, and, therefore, we will unconsciously choose behaviors that put us at risk for conflict. This can accelerate to a degree that brings unimaginable harm into our lives. At that point then, we are faced with tidal waves of emotion, and at that moment, we must feel it, whether we want to or not. Even then, it can be assigned, since there is no limit to the ability of the human mind to deny reality.

In our language, we have such expressions as "gut feelings," "I can't stomach that," "That gripes me," "I take that to heart," "Getting our back up," "heartache." There is good cause for the presence of these feelings.

Our minds are our gatherers, mediators, synthesizers, and interpreters for all the stimuli coming from our seven senses of sight, sound, touch, taste, smell, intuition, and attitude. Each and every cell in our bodies originally had the generic potential to take part in producing, detecting, and responding to one or many of these stimuli.

Each cell in our bodies has the generic encoding for human behavior that, throughout the past millions of years, has been, and still is, the species-specific guide for the development of each Homo sapiens to be able to live interdependently in a cooperative community. Consequently, we do sense and feel in our bones, and potentially in every cell in our bodies, those deviant behaviors that, in general, are threatening the continued survival of the human species. The strongest of these feelings felt throughout our bodies is the sense of rejection.

It is hard to imagine that any person considers lying to be the best way to relate to others, but it is most devastating when we lie to ourselves. When we feel that we must lie to ourselves, our self-esteem goes down, because we are behaving contrary to natural law. Natural law is that part of our awareness that is intuitive. More especially, it is that part of inborn knowingness that is encoded in the genes of every cell in our bodies. In the past billion or so years, every species developed and evolved survival techniques. These behavior patterns became ever more complex as animals developed from one-celled creatures to organisms of trillions of cells.

We also evolved internal defense systems, our immune systems, which allow kindred cells to recognize each other, and thereby welcome and protect allies, while fighting and destroying foreign cells and organisms. Every animal also developed a code of species behavior, so like life forms could coexist and procreate. This encoding in every cell of all living substance also includes a distinct species pattern that is observable and discernible.

We, as members of the human race, have millions of generations of successful ancestors. As Homo sapiens, we have evolved a subconscious awareness, which is the extension and expansion of this intercellular recognition. This, for us as individuals, can be termed, cognizance, for this concept of recognition and cooperation expands to relationships in our families and our tribes and can be thought of as natural law. At a personal level, this is more commonly termed, "gut feelings," because when we willfully overrule our subconscious awareness, we will get discomforting feelings, usually in the abdomen. This occurs, if we have emotionally developed beyond the age of three, whenever we are being untruthful to ourselves or breaking any part of the natural law encased in our genes concerning conduct with others. We will be reminded internally that we have broken natural law. An emotionally mature adult will retain the ability to perceive these strong gut feelings. The Ten Commandments could be cited as an early codification of these natural laws.

Rather than having interactions with others, the newborn infant is primarily influenced within himself, because he is primarily directed by his genetic encoding. As he matures emotionally, he becomes increasingly aware that his greater good is related to a reciprocal support of others. Unless he is blocked and emotionally stunted, a strong feeling of responsibility will start kicking in at about the age of thirty-six months.

If, in early childhood, we are scolded, criticized, or rejected as we attempt to behave according to our gut feelings, then we become greatly stressed. When this occurs time and time again, we are forced to withdraw inwardly by shutting down our own native drives. If our families not only consider our normal, exuberant, infantile traits to be unacceptable, but also mandate that they be replaced by controlled, contrite behaviors, then our troublesome presence is kept out of their way. Consequently, we are less bothersome. As a reactive result, our ability to recognize our intuitive feelings becomes blunted. However, we cannot permanently extinguish this intuitive awareness, for it still resides in every cell of our bodies.

The main issue is trust. Within ourselves, we have the ability to recapitulate our own history by retrieving it from the permanent archives residing in our subconscious minds. Even more importantly, we have the capacity, through our sixth sense, intuition, to know our own innermost drives. This natural design feature makes it certain that we are the only ones in this world who have the insight potential to thoroughly understand ourselves.

In a protected and safe environment, the use of relaxation and meditation techniques makes intuitive awareness available to us. These processes can temporarily allow us to let down our defenses. Many people seek enlightenment with the unfounded belief that the process requires magic or mystery. We avoid any thought of mystery when we seek what we know to be there. Thoroughly relaxed in a state of tranquility, we afford ourselves the opportunity to tune into our inner selves. Through meditation, our goal is to be temporarily released from all of our defenses and temporarily free of the need for explanations and rationalizations of our beliefs, and thereby, regain an understanding of our innermost selves. That is, we can get in touch and be in accord with our ever so rich emotional inheritance and inborn drives. As a practical point, any time we are in defensive postures for any reason, we compromise or shut off much understanding of both the past and the future.

Automatic defenses are stored in the reptilian

and limbic parts of our brains. When we perceive a threat, we instantly let loose an orchestrated execution of conjoined defenses that come from our brain stems and midbrains. All defense posturing is proportional to the perceived threat. Our midbrains not only activate all of our bodily organs, but also modulate total coordination of voluntary motor muscles for the current survival effort. When we enact these defenses, we simultaneously preclude most cortical thought. This instantaneous activation almost obviates the chance of electing more advantageous action for the future. Also, by the short-circuiting of higher centers, we simultaneously prevent ourselves from accessing our intuitive inspirational thoughts, which could be advantageous and beneficial for actions in the present.

The common defense of argumentation can be recognized as a most subtle form of anger and resistance. Defenses are evident when we feel compelled to explain "why" to justify any current behaviors or beliefs. The use of such words as "try," "should," "ought," and "must," all presage lies that we are about to tell. These words are used to placate others, covering up efforts to force ourselves into doing what we inwardly resent. It is impossible for us to like ourselves when we lie, because it causes us to feel stress. The disclaimer here is that if our emotional personalities are arrested before the age of three, then the natural phenomenon of feeling responsibility does not develop.

These uneasy feelings in our innards come whenever we are about to command ourselves to compromise our self-esteem. When we are transgressing, or trying to be other than who we are, there are deeper and more profound reactions that inwardly excite intuitive "sinking feelings," or "gut feelings." When a person is committing what has been labeled as "sin," he is transgressing a rule set down by him or by an alleged authoritarian figure or group. In self-protection, he "steels" himself, or feels guilt, for what reaction will result from doing something wrong.

The most common sins are prefaced by the words "should," "ought," "have to," "must," and "try." We do not "have to do" anything in this world—however we may starve or get punished for non-compliance. "Should," "ought," "have to," "must," and "try," are all imperative commands that we use on ourselves to outwardly attempt to appease our commanders (parents or older siblings) who, in reality, often may be long since dead. In these acts of subservience, we are behaving as if we are still the victims of our fathers, mothers, older siblings, or whomever. The big sin is that we lie to ourselves. Originally, because we are in fear of the consequences and are young and vulnerable, we adopt the adjustment belief that we have to tell people what they want to hear. Even though we do not want to carry out their orders, we grudgingly comply.

Should we desire to mature emotionally, we may elect to take charge and choose not to be victims of ourselves. Any time we electively choose to no longer serve as volunteers, our emotional cost will be initially high and then vastly reduced. It is initially high, because we have to face, embrace, and lose the fear of not being loved and accepted that controlled us in the first place, and which is clearly residing in our subconscious minds. If we are willing to own that fear as our own and feel it completely, then it gradually dissolves forever. We may do the same tasks or follow similar courses, but acting by our choice, we are no longer lying or cutting ourselves down. When our actions are in accord with our gut feelings, we avoid activating parts or the whole of bodily defense systems.

In various evangelistic religious groups, the

THEODORE J. SMITH, M.D.

Internal Medicine - Hypnoanalysis

725 S. 49th St.
Tacoma, WA 98408

Tel (253) 476-8549
Fax (253) 476-85??

charismatic leader proffers an invitation to come forward and be saved. The meaning of being saved was a mystery to us for fifty years. Finally, it became clear what this concept is all about. This seductive routine of the persuasive leader is a promise that he, the evangelist, will relieve us sinners of personal responsibility—our burden will be lifted. We will renounce our personal efforts of self-jurisdiction. Then, because we are no longer responsible, the implication is that we have cleared emotional pathways, so that the leader can take over direction of our lives by substituting his organizational control over our emotional behaviors or thought processes. In these conversions, we submit by agreeing to stop proffering and defending our own views, and instead, we align our beliefs with those of our new group, merely turning over control of our lives to this new outside force. We become one with this great body of people and join them in being defended and controlled by the fatherly figure. We assume protective dependency by espousing the evangelist's beliefs. The implication is that we are incompetent to determine our own futures for ourselves.

Surrendering our inane defenses, numerous old beliefs, and prejudices is the essential initial step to enlightenment. Surrendering control is necessary, but in no way should we replace our personal defense structures with the domineering control of another person or system. True emotional maturity requires relinquishing all control by replacing it with our conscious self-management. When we intuitively tune into our very individual templates that are inherent in our genetic DNA, we become our own managing directors in accordance with our self-esteem and natural law. In communal conversion to a missionary group, we submit by agreeing to stop promoting and defending our own static views; in their place we revise our beliefs as we give control of our lives to this ever present outside force.

In contrast, enlightenment involves relinquishing the control of "doing things my own way" and instead, becoming our own highest authorities. Using open minds, we can tune into our intuition. We can elect the ideal direction, which is the path that is uniquely suited for fulfillment of our templates to live out more fully the potentials encoded in our DNA. Communication of our minds, spirits, and souls with the Infinite Source will come, not through our thoughtful reasoning and logic, but by intuitive cognizance, as we learn to communicate with our innermost resources. That is, we simply know things because we know. This primary being and knowing level is a common denominator with which we can relate to all other humans. Also, at this level, we have available to us our full potentials for creative activities.

The core need for our salvation is to be liberated from ourselves. Until now, we have had static, restricting attitudes, which have been our bondage and have prevented us from revising our beliefs in ourselves and have limited our understanding of others. Other people will always put limits on what we can do, but as adults, we are the primary ones who continue to put limits on how we feel about ourselves.

In the final countdown, we are the ones who need to accept ourselves. A Christian tenet is, "Jesus loves and accepts you." In a sense, that is unimportant, because Jesus accepts all mankind; no one can earn acceptance. Our true need is to accept ourselves. We suggest that, as the next step, we acquaint ourselves with every aspect of the natural laws that are inherent within us. Our goal is to synchronize with the driving life force that is innate within us. This will allow us to mature, becoming warm, open, and accepting adults.

This view in no way precludes or excludes the existence of a fantastic organizing drive, or Higher Intelligence, which has set the whole universe in progress in an organized way and has formed our genetic templates. Reality, then, is living the fundamental truth that our own DNA contains all the knowledge and direction needed to live full and graceful lives, and that this direction is accessed through our intuition.

Changing Our Beliefs

Once we realize that all perception is projection, or in other words, all that we allow ourselves to see is determined by our beliefs, which precede perception, then our natural desire is to expand those beliefs and redefine them. We want to allow greater perception and, eventually, come to know our filters completely, which is extremely rare.

There are several methods we can use to uncover and revise our beliefs in ways that are more favorable to expanded, joyful lives. One method that we've detailed in this book is hypnotic age reenactment, utilizing trained guides who direct us to clearly recall the emotional events during which we formed our most fundamental beliefs about self-worth, self-esteem, and our places in the order of mankind. By revisiting these intensely emotional experiences and reviewing the conclusions we drew at those times, we, with our adult perspectives in the age reenactment sessions, will have the option to imagine different treatment from our caretakers, resulting in different outcomes, and we can draw more insightful conclusions about the reality of life, which then become our living realities based on new and revised beliefs. This method is very potent and effective. It does, however, require suitable environments and competent guides. Because of these requirements, it is not available to everyone at all times.

In addition to age re-enactment and hypnosis, there are other methods that can affect our beliefs. The first recommendation would be Transcendental Meditation, a mental technique unlike other meditations, in that it does not require concentration or contemplation; it is without content and yet, it is profound. This meditation technique allows the mind to systematically experience subtler and subtler levels of thought, transcending the conscious thinking level to arrive at the finest thinking level and then transcending that level to deliver a clear experience of beingness, our own true Self. The technique produces a state of profound relaxation, and this, by itself, allows the natural intelligence encoded in our genes to rearrange many of our beliefs in our physiology, and to express, more and more, our inherent potentials. Transcendental Meditation, by itself, is not a solution to all problems; however, it is profoundly beneficial for health, as has been amply documented, and it has tremendous value in helping us on our way to revising our belief systems to be as reality-based as possible.

Next, we would recommend deep tissue work. The belief system is held in the unconscious mind, which is the body. All emotions are things that are felt; that means they are sensations, and that means they are felt by the body, so the body is the seat of all emotions. If the body is physically restructured, there will be an effect on the emotions and the beliefs that underlie them. In particular, the system of Rolfing is helpful in restructuring our bodies in the direction of our natural potentials. There is a normal, natural human posture ordained by our genes, from which many of us have deviated, sometimes very significantly. As a result, we may not stand and walk comfortably. This will have a parallel in our internal emotional state, since our minds and bodies are intimately related, and our emotions are directly stored in our bodies. Rolfing systematically stretches the connective tissue to allow for normal posture, which is helpful for health as well as for progress in the spiritual dimension of realigning our belief systems with our highest potentials. Most cities have trained Rolfers, and these can be found in the Yellow Pages or on the Internet.

Yoga is also a form of bodywork that stretches the connective tissue for the same purpose of allowing us to realign our posture and, at the same time, our emotions with our own natural, highest form.

We would also highly recommend the method of Classical Five-Element Acupuncture, as taught by Drs. J.R. and J.B. Worsley. J.R. Worsley discovered this ancient method of healing while traveling in the Orient and spent fifty years teaching and practicing this unique system of medicine. Although the medicine originated in ancient China, where it had been practiced for thousands of years, it is not currently practiced there.

The common method of acupuncture used in China today was largely formulated by the Communists as a formulary system, using the acupuncture points in patterns to treat specific disease entities. This method of acupuncture persists in China now, and is known in the

West as Traditional Chinese Medicine.

Classical Five-Element Acupuncture uses the same acupuncture points; however, the method of diagnosis, the method of selecting the points, the method of needling the points, and the intention are totally different. In Classical Five-Element Acupuncture, the points are used to treat our spirits to correct our most fundamental imbalances, bringing physical transformations that can modify our belief systems.

It may seem odd to think of a physical procedure, such as acupuncture, changing our belief systems. However, it makes perfect sense when we consider that the beliefs are stored in the body and connected with emotional experiences, which are also stored in the body. For this reason, a method of acupuncture that finds the most fundamental imbalance, and corrects it energetically, assists greatly in our progress toward revising our limiting beliefs. With regular treatments of Classical Five-Element Acupuncture, we begin to feel tremendously more like ourselves, meaning that, more and more, we are aligning ourselves to our inherent, human genetic potentials for awareness, joy, love, creativity, harmony, and health.

More on Changing Our Belief Systems

Changing any of our routines, habits, behaviors, or emotional reactions is sometimes very difficult, for all these areas are protected by well-rehearsed automatic defenses. Learned and practiced routines are in place to enable us to run our lives more or less automatically, because our organized routines eliminate the minute, voluntary control needed for finely tuned actions. These programs create our private protection, for their unity constitutes our very own personal safe places. The structuring of these reactions has allowed us to remain alive until now.

Established routines have provided us with regulated functions, without the need for millions of minute-to-minute and month-to-month decisions.

However, each time we exercise these habits and automatic defenses, we must bypass the neural circuits of our higher cognitive thought. Slavishly operating our lives blots out the opportunities to experience possibly fuller lives, because routines preclude new choices to mature our attitudes and thereby modify our behavior.

The accumulation and revision of our beliefs forms and reshapes our attitudes. Habit patterns are not age related, but attitudes are. Our attitudes toward life, living, our self-worth, and our relationships to others are the products of coping with experiences which have occurred at specific times throughout our lives. Our perceptions of each initial incident is limited by the stimuli that we receive from our seven senses, and those perceptions are determined and limited by the developmental state of our central nervous system at the time. Our capability for forming sophisticated defenses, or beliefs, is restricted by our abilities and by our voluntary openness to take in and process all information available.

There is a chronological order for the development and adoption of beliefs and attitudes. The first is cognizance, which is the inborn, genetically based intuition and basic start-up belief of, "I belong in this world and no one else matters."

The next to develop, in early infancy, is anger, which is inborn as a survival technique. It can be a primary adjustment in his environment when an infant experiences lack of respect for his individuality; anger then becomes his primary equalizer.

Early in infancy, we have feelings of worthiness or lack thereof, and self-placement in the human pecking order occurs. Also in infancy, we have the preservation of fears that are passed down genetically in our DNA from the accumulated experiences of our ancestors, such as the fears of exposure to high places and snakes. We can also acquire fears at this time learned from personal exposure to traumatic encounters, and the formation of their routine defenses. Routines and habit patterns start in infancy.

The next layer to develop, in early childhood, is more complex belief formation. Initial belief about any observation, occurrence, or hearsay may be tentative. The first impression is important because it gives us a basis upon which to compare and evaluate additional incoming collateral data.

Later in infancy, up to thirty-six months, fixed beliefs form. As soon as we defend or rationalize any position, our minds are closed, at least temporarily. If, in spite of any new and varying valid information concerning our beliefs, we choose to continuously defend our dogma, we are then behaving rigidly, as if we are already senile.

We will never know everything about anything. New information may support what we already know, and thereby strengthen our resolve, but more likely, when we accept added information, our beliefs will automatically be revised to some degree. Our defenses of viewpoints escalate roughly proportionately to our fear when considering new information.

When insects and so-called lesser animals are threatened, their defenses are driven by their genetically established responses. Man, with the most highly developed cerebral cortex, has the greatest ability to evaluate and then choose or veto each action, and thereby, modify his attitude and subsequent behavior. Man, above all other animals, has this unique ability to determine his own quality of life. However, the number and nature of our personality arrests limit this upward improvement. Protective emotional bulkheads mandate rigidly fixed habit patterns, which greatly limit our freedom of choice.

Understanding the Terrorist's Behavior

Understanding an act of human behavior requires that we focus upon the factors that cause another person's attitudes. Each individual is born with a set of attitudes and behaviors, which, from birth onward, are modified and augmented. Each person creates his own personality by adopting attitudes about himself and his individuality or lack of personal identity. In infancy and early childhood, the developing brain has increasing capacity to evaluate and understand the self-image that it accepts as attitude. When first adopted, each defense is both logical and reasonable, but only in terms of the infant's limited cognitive power.

Human nature is such that we try to identify and assign "motives" to every person's actions. We seek to contrive these motives in logical contemporary terms, but our actions are seldom purely logical, because, in general, we act first and think later. And this "thinking later" is generally to justify the action we have just taken. This is because we are basically creatures of learned emotional responses and habits. Logic is a come-lately evolutionary acquisition. Learning from experience and defense have been our evolutionary keys to survival. In order to comprehend the mechanism motivating the formation of beliefs and defenses, we need to examine the workings of the human brain.

When we consider the motive for a current behavior, we take at face value the apparent motive, which seems most logical. Then we assume what is an enormous fallacy because most of our actions and basic behaviors are controlled not by selection, using our conscious minds, but rather, by reliance on our subconscious minds to instantly replay past behavior that saved our lives. The motive and deep underlying cause is months and years removed from the current threatening event. If we examine and know the motivating mechanism that resides in the archives of our brains, realizing that these survival techniques are constantly active in our subconscious minds, then, in retrospect, our actions and the behaviors of every other person become rational and/or reasonable, not necessarily for the present, but always in terms of those ancient threats, when we first experienced a similar situation long, long ago. Each of our individual defense reactions was stimulated by a perceived grave threat, which in turn, caused the founding of a single new belief and attitude. Discovering our underlying emotional assumptions is simple, though challenging. We have only to examine our own behavior under stress and ask, "What would a person have to believe to act this way?" We are often astonished to find out what our real, operational, emotional beliefs really are, and they are usually much farther from our idealized self-portraits than we care to admit.

It is true that our total brains are in control. But the discretionary parts of our minds, our neo-cortexes, are but minor and inconstant contributors to our bodies' current total reactions. Most of our supposed thought is merely justifying decisions that we have already made.

It is a fact that we can create thoughts and voluntarily activate our skeletal muscles to perform individual tasks, but even in these actions our subconscious minds automatically fine-tune and coordinate muscle tensions and simultaneously regulate our bodies' organ functioning. In total, our subconscious minds are responsible for 95% of all our physical activities and attitudes.

All our lives, by exposures to stimuli and practices, we have been training our subconscious minds to semiautomatically run our whole systems, relying on habit patterns and defenses. In our present state of development, we do not need to command every little detail. We do make moment to moment selections of gross habit patterns, acts, and performances that we have practiced and done before. These actions are merely those of repeating routines while changing only minor variations and creating little that is new. Life has to be this way, because our superior thinking brains, our neocortexes, could not handle the millions and millions of instantaneous and simultaneous decisions necessary for the machinery of our bodies to run smoothly.

The problem is that there is a dichotomy between the behavior as ordered by our conscious minds and the more or less mandatory behavior and beliefs directed by our subconscious minds. Except in the brain-damaged person, all behaviors are entirely appropriate, when defensive behavior is viewed as age-related and considered only when it first appears in its infantile or childish proper age setting. Considering time and developmental age, all actions are originated by good logical reasoning.

Our conscious minds can consider the past, the present, and the future. Our subconscious minds consider that all the past is still the present, and there is only the present for every consideration. Every bit of information recorded in our subconscious minds is inscribed in precise impressions, as if it is happening right now. For logical consideration, the initial challenges and threats that happened many years ago, when we were infants, remain fresh and active in our subconscious minds. The conscious memory of events may be gone and forgotten, but the details of those occurrences are retained in the exact impressions recorded in our subconscious minds, and they are alive and active. Computer science has adopted a similar scheme. That is, the subconscious mind is like the hard drive, and the working conscious mind is similar to the RAM.

A gross extenuation of this phenomenon is in the tribal attitude of the indigenous warring peoples in the

Middle East. They regard historical invasions and ancient killings of their tribes as if they are still happening. They preserve these mental pictures, which sustain their current attitude of victimhood, which in turn, continues to command their present behavior. Considering their ancient mind-set, which is now transferred to modern times, makes their present behavior of revenge and reparation somewhat understandable.

Returning consideration from races and tribes back to individuals, we have the same mechanism. This condition arises because automatic defenses are the product of the two more primitive parts of our nervous systems, the limbic brain and the midbrain. By design, the primitive parts of our brains have the primary purpose of creating avoidance-defense behaviors. They do prepare us for the future by holding us in readiness to act exactly as we did so successfully in the past. These maneuvers are activated automatically whenever there is the slightest hint of the recurrence of the threat of that danger we experienced previously. When reactivated, the defense is entirely the same as it was at the exact moment of its formation. All defenses are maintained in readiness for the future, but they are not fully running until some vaguely perceived similar threat stimulates them to turn on.

Our most potent and dramatic defenses are formed in infancy and early childhood when our developing brains are impotent. During these early periods, our brains have a very limited range of responses. If the sanctity of our individuality is overwhelmed by the potential magnitude of the threats, then we form our most ardent defenses and attitudes that last the rest of our lives. As infants, we are truly victims of circumstances and the people close to us. Consequently, the defenses we form are logical; that is, logical for the limited amount of brain function we have at that time. Our defenses are further restricted by our limited ability to perceive and interpret the stimuli that come streaming in by way of all our senses.

Today as adults, we are individuals who have inadvertently been stunted by emotional arrests in infancy, and we maintain and continue the same attitudes of vulnerability that we experienced in very early life. Whenever we perceive similar threats, we activate and replay our childhood feelings of vulnerability, and we automatically and totally reactivate our defense systems in precisely the same manner.

However, the intellectual parts of our nervous systems are now mature. Consequently, we compound all our acquired fears with primitive experiences and outwardly express and execute the same defense mechanisms, but currently, we do so in a revised, sophisticated manner. However, depending upon our overall emotional maturity, we as Homo sapiens, have the power and prerogative to temporarily veto and suppress these automatic behaviors.

Infantile behavior is exemplified by the O.J. Simpson murder case. Without making excuses, if we consider O.J. Simpson's primitive defense system, then his unbridled rage and the act of murder were entirely normal. O.J.'s emotional development was arrested and stabilized at a one-year-old level. As a physical adult, O.J. chooses to use, or not to use, his highest intellectual centers in selectively vetoing immature emotional drives of his subconscious mind. He can temporarily behave as a very intelligent man, possessing tremendous athlete prowess. However, when his buttons are pushed, his behavior can turn from that of an entirely normal adult to that of the enraged infant who resides within him.

In comparison, almost everyone has seen a

three-month-old infant lying in his crib feeling deprived, getting angry, and turning his anger to rage. He is thrashing about, turning blue, and striking into the air aimlessly. Will we try to reason with him? Now, we can consider an athletic adult who emotionally has chosen to be provoked and is acting like a standard three-month-old enraged infant—will we try to reason with him?

The reason for this personality arrest follows a very standard common pattern. If, as infants, our vital dependency needs for nurture are not met, then we reflectively form defenses to maintain and protect what little individuality we have acquired. Now that we are adults, this retained-infant-inside is still nagging for fulfillment. That is, in order to develop the potential that is encoded in our personal genes, we have a burning and driving need for fulfillment and acceptance. Initially, a nurturing person must administer support and acceptance. For years, Nicole Simpson probably serviced O.J. by catering to his primitive needs, but eventually, she tired of playing the role of his mother— she wanted him to "grow-up." As a result, he felt abandoned, like a baby left alone. Nicole's rejecting him, possibly for another man, caused O.J. to let his active, infantile anger go unchecked; feelings of abandonment and jealousy caused him to destroy what he could not possess.

Every attitude is age related. Behavior for each attitude is more or less standard. When properly age-related, every attitude and behavior is entirely normal. The terrorist has been schooled in his tribal, generic fears. Emotionally, he is a three-month-old baby with needs, but no conscience. Consequently, he can wantonly kill civilians with no evidence of regret, because he is merely flailing his arms out in every direction, which is entirely proper behavior for an enraged infant who feels totally unappreciated. There is no way that we can make a three-month-old feel guilty or cause him to have any regrets for what he soils or destroys.

As a society, our universal problem is our expectation that adults should exhibit only adult behavior, which could happen only if all people were totally ruled by their conscious minds, rather than dominated by their subconscious attitudes.

A person's immature behavior should not be excused because of personality arrests that were inflicted on him in infancy. Every person has some awareness of his shortcomings and relative impairments. Likewise, every alcoholic or drug addict and every angry person has, deep inside of himself, the awareness that he has a personality problem. We must never make excuses for him, or we become part of the problem; rather we should require him to do something for himself.

If, during our first two years, we are treated with respect and encouraged to become the persons whose potentials are encoded in our genes, then our individualities are our very own. If instead of being encouraged to be individuals, we are forced to play the only roles our possessive, highly opinionated parents will allow; then, we are true victims. Islamic fundamentalists are taught that the very paper on which the Koran is written is more valuable that human life, especially their own, and that they can get acceptance and glory only in the hereafter. If, in order to exist in our families or tribes, we are forced to accept imposed self-images of worthlessness, then we may always feel that we are victims of others and their authority. No normal human being wants to be owned and dominated.

Subjugation of our individualities can and mostly likely does cause residual infantile anger and rage to become a predominant individual attitude. As helpless victims, the assumption of anger and rage will be the only experiential, safe venue in which we can demand some degree of self-expression and forcefully bid for respect. As adults, we can be possessed by this seething resentment for never having had our dependency needs fulfilled, and we are then dangerous to society. In twisted logic, therefore, people that we perceive to be keeping us down (as they did in very early infancy) are our enemies and must be destroyed, so that they cannot continue to oppress us in any way in the future.

We find an extension of this same phenomenon—feeling inadequate and unimportant—in people who form tightly knit groups, organized primarily for protection of beliefs and principles. They relinquish personal freedom for what they view as security. After the terrorist attack on the World Trade Center in New York, a group of political leaders and college students in Kuwait were interviewed. They were basically anti-American and favored more strict Moslem clerical laws somewhat similar to Afghanistan's. They stated their reason for desiring this closed society is that it made their families secure. That is, everyone knows his place and the whole society will punish those who dare to deviate from approved behavior. A corollary principle is: The more inadequate we feel ourselves to be, the more we need to surrender ourselves to and espouse radical groups.

In all groups of religious worshipers, there seem to develop sects of reform and ultraconservatives. Characteristically, the conservatives go more and more by the book—more rigid rules with less and less individual interpretation. In ancient Egypt, the worshipers gave up their individualities to work almost like slaves, so that they might join the Pharaoh in his ascent to the eternal hereafter. In the Middle Ages, the Catholics held the inquisition to eliminate those who did not follow their strict decrees. In America, the Protestants shunned, and even burned at the stake, those who did not think or act in accordance with their religious beliefs. Today in Israel, the ultra-conservative believers will possibly destroy the democracy. The ultra conservatives of Islam seek to reinstate the religious rules and laws of the Middle Ages, as set forth by Mohammed.

This is where the big rift develops. When we, in the United States, hold that all individuals have free choice to pursue happiness, then we must necessarily question or rebuke highly codified demands for belief and outside direction of all the actions of our lives. In their view, we are Satans and must be destroyed for even thinking about questioning the authority of the Koran.

Terrorists, then, are groups of people united by emotional developmental delay at an infantile age, who possess adult bodies and intellectual abilities, which they use in service of their underlying rage against any entity that even gently evokes the repression of their individualities that occurred in infancy. Theirs is a subconscious, emotional attitude, not alterable by discussion, and their combined abilities at war make them dangerous indeed.

The basic struggle in the world today, and for the future, is between regimentation and the inherent individuality and value of each person.

The Controlled Mind

We can recognize controlled minds by the attitudes that cause individuals to automatically jump to the defense of their dogma. There are varying degrees to which each of us has shut off our cognitive thinking, because we regard our beliefs as life-saving defenses, and thereby exclude any reassessment by our discriminating higher thought processes. Controlled minds can be manipulated into argument by the mere suggestion of a challenge to entrenched beliefs. In behavior manipulation, we can stir up the anger and rage response, which is maintained in resentful readiness, whenever we push the right buttons. The buttons may involve physical contact or spoken or implied words. Any attitude of fear advertises that a person is ready for subjective control by his tormentors or by con-artists.

The more subtle and devious manipulators learn to implant suggestions, which become temporary beliefs, and then skillfully challenge these beliefs, so that we defend them against any onslaught. The more we defend any dogma or fixed ideas, the more we will stake our lives on any assumed premises. Any challenges or suggestions which contain slight deviations from our fixed beliefs will instantly trigger our defenses. At those times, impulses to action bypass all critical thinking by short-circuiting stimulation that would be electrically routed through our neocortexes. In this defensive mode, we preclude any possibility of the reception or adoption of new information which might alter our firm beliefs. In short, we are all mind controlled whenever we can be induced to act without open consideration of the suggestions, and there are individuals and groups, such as cults, who are very adept at engineering this type of subconscious behavior.

Brainwashing

The beliefs that we hold are founded on the information that we had at the time of their adoption. They become additional parts of our attitudes, comprising our identities and our self-images. Commonly, we identify people by what they do—their occupations—rather than who they are. The total collection of our beliefs includes our self-images, our self-esteem, and all our learned habits and defenses. These beliefs form our attitudes, not only toward our work, but more especially toward who we are, and are the presentations of our personas that we project to the whole world. Our attitudes also determine our automatic responses, unless we choose to exercise willful control or modification. With our preset attitudes, we create and stimulate our emotions according to our expectations.

By accumulating valid information about an individual's past behavior, we can derive a picture of each man's belief about himself and the strength of his self-identity. Also, from his history, sometimes from even a number of small snippets of it, we can gain a good, qualified appraisal of his susceptibility to suggestion and his need for identity coming from outside of himself—any deficiency in individuality that must be filled by associations with another person, as in marriage or membership in an organization, group, or gang.

When prospecting for a convert to our own ideas or ecumenical groups, we should identify an individual who has a weak self-identity and self-esteem, as this type of individual is most likely in need of shelter for his nakedness of un-identifiablility. He presents himself as eager and willing to enter into a supportive association. Any alliance will vicariously give the position of respect and support he earnestly seeks.

After identifying the prospective convert, we establish rapport by our show of approval of what he is doing, wearing, or saying. When his self-identity is fragile, we can expect that this approval will be taken by him as acceptance of him as a person. Next, by introducing him to our group, we confirm further approval. When he appears to be ready, we encourage him to commingle with us and our group. We call to his attention that he has a strong commonality with our group. Then, we flatter him, telling him that he is cool and belongs with our great bunch of guys.

Next, we further strengthen a strong comradeship with our members. If the candidate perceives that he is better accepted here than anywhere else, he will openly go along with the group's credo and its mission. If, on the other hand, we learn that our prospect has a very strong self-image and faith in himself, we will find it difficult or impossible to recruit him for our group or to further our agenda.

From the very first sight, we get hints. Does he wear the clothes, jewelry, and hairstyle that are currently so popular with the "in" crowd? Does his speech echo the current street language? Does he smoke or do the popular local drug? The less individualism that he has, the more our group will indirectly be able to give him clues to follow in order to become one of us. Thereby, we create the illusion that we afford him a degree of acceptance greater than he expects from anyone else.

To understand this person's background, we need to study the dynamics of acceptance. Simply stated, if during our first three years, we fail to establish good feelings about our self-worth, then lack of respect for ourselves will be included in our lifelong self-images. These self-images persist unless we engage in some effective self-help programs. If we reach the second three years of our lives possessing weak identities, we are forced to seek our identities through alliances with other persons or groups, who will define who we are. As an essential part of our survival as humans, we need, most of all, to feel accepted. The need for acceptance from without is especially strong during the first six years of our lives, and instinctively, we know that we need to be accepted at that time, because we cannot live alone unattended. Acceptance, especially self-acceptance, can be considered as an ultimate goal of our lives. Life's ultimate achievement is to completely accept ourselves, by ourselves, free of all pretenses. Ultimately, the reality is that only self-acceptance is fulfillment. Moreover, we cannot accept any others more than we accept ourselves.

The whole mind control game hinges upon getting the prospective convert to interpret approval for what he does as acceptance for who he is.

We desire that other people accept us, but what we can expect to receive from others is limited. Their ability to accept anyone is almost immutable—a self-restrained condition that we have no power to change. That is, each person has his own personal limitations, which, because of his learned fears, curtail and prohibit complete acceptance of us. These prejudices are his alone, and there is nothing we can do that will solve his problem for him. For instance, if we are genuine females, and if he is afraid and hates all women, there is nothing that we can do that will necessarily affect his beliefs. Or, sometimes our mothers accept us only as they did when we were children. They do not accept us as adults, because they continue to regard us condescendingly, as if we were still small children.

Acceptance from birth to about the age of three must come from outside of us—preferably from our parents. By their acceptance, our parents affirm that we are not part of them, but rather, that we are equal individuals—equal in being, not doing. When our parents fail to acknowledge or even disdain some of our natural attributes and normal behaviors, we predictably do not like those parts of our total characters. Only with initial affirmation can we continue to believe in ourselves with all of our individual characteristics. By thirty-six-months, we should be confident enough to begin to accept and love others, but our ability to love will be in direct correlation to the assurance that we feel is extended by our parents in accepting us and all of our characteristics.

If we, as members of groups, gangs, organizations, or cults, are out to recruit new members, we observe behaviors, looking for the individual who parallels our own attitudes, for we can expect him to share some beliefs similar to ours. Next, we ask him to join in some of our activities—smoking, small talk with the lowest content that attracts him—anything that will give the impression that we approve of him. If our approval of his behavior and speech causes him to believe that he is better accepted by us and our group than by anybody else, this is where he will want to be.

In general discussion, we search to gain a sense of some of his most affirmed beliefs. Those prejudices that most closely coincide with ours, we strongly support, and commiserate—ain't it awful. When he is comfortable, we introduce some of the devotees of our group or cult, rather casually at first. Further, we commingle parts of our agenda with the discussion of his firm beliefs, as if these premises were directly connected. After a while, when he goes along with these two ideas in tandem, we challenge his firm, basic beliefs, and thereby, encourage him to defend himself more and more. When he is emotionally in defense, his critical thinking mind isn't alert. That is the cue to start attacking his basic beliefs in tandem with our suggestions.

Now it is time to switch back to strongly support his program to feign that he has won us over. As we commiserate, we induce him to join in to defend our special program. The more furiously he defends our dogma, the more his thinking and critical mind have been bypassed. Also, by observing his dedicated defense, we know this apostle will be eager to espouse our great cause. This protocol is used instructively by all great recruiters, salesmen, con artists, and cult leaders. It exists in human culture from time immemorial, and it succeeds because it is based on the innate structures of the human mind and personality. It is the method by which all powerful groups attract and maintain their members. It is only those individuals with strong senses of self-worth who are immune to its allure.

Frankness and Reality

The main purpose of the book is to bring the reader to reality; that is, to see situations as they truly are. Reality is frank; we arrive at reality when we mentally delete all pretense, explanations, and excuses. When we are dealing with reality, we need to be fully aware of how we feel and make no rationalizations for anyone's inappropriate behavior. All current behaviors are the way they are because this moment is just what each individual, consciously or subconsciously, wants it to be. We avoid any explanations or justifications to ourselves. We discount how we feel, what we think we deserve, or what we consider is fair. We make no excuses of any kind—the world just is. We think and describe our surroundings as objectively as we can. We make constant and continuing analysis, but we make no judgments.

Any attempt to justify another person's behavior signifies that we have problems similar to his, and furthermore, we are probably not yet ready to seek and explore the origin of our problems in that area. Reality must prevail in order for us to begin to accept any resolution of those problems. A goodly portion of our social order is based on making concessions, giving allowances, and making excuses rather than facing the problems. Nature's reality is that there is no "fudge factor," and, there is only one reason that we do anything, and it is because we want to. Except in the brain-damaged individual, all behaviors are merely normal human behaviors; that is, if we totally ignore chronological age and seek to identify the emotional age of an untoward behavior, we can readily identify at what chronological age the specific activity would be normal, or at least acceptable. According to that observed behavior, we can readily age-relate standard attitudes.

We cannot change the basic laws by which Nature is constituted. Likewise, we may rearrange some DNA in chromosomes, but there will be limits on how we can manipulate living cells. We have almost unlimited potential—more potential that we can develop in our lifetimes. Our finest achievements will be the development of personas that are in accord with the potentials encoded in our genes. Any attempt that we make ourselves, or that is mandated by our caretakers, to be different and therefore, contrived persons with different personalities, will cause us to be out of reality; that is, we will be emotionally dysfunctional.

Our reality is to be our own separate individuals.

Case History—Jill

This case report concerns Jill, an attractive, very bright young lady of twenty-three, whose apartment has consistently been a housekeeping disaster. This lack of attention to orderliness and appearance seems limited to this one area of her emotional life. Obviously, this behavior is out of character for her general social adjustment, and it defies adult logic.

Let us examinine Jill's behavior. If this behavior does not seem to be adult behavior, at what age would such behavior be accepted as normal? It has to be at a very young age—all the way back to a time when she was not able to be, or expected to be, tidy, concerned about the appearance of her immediate surroundings, or discomforted with living in an accumulated mess.

Obviously, we are talking about an infant who, at birth, accepts the family home in which she is born, whether it is a cave, a shack, or a palace. It is safe to assume that her attitude is normal for a baby. However, continuing this attitude into adulthood represents an extension of an arrest, which occurred very early in Jill's normal, emotional development. It represents a protection—a protective emotional bulkhead that she has carried forward from her infancy. If her emotional stream had been allowed to mature normally, she would have, at the age of three, started to assume a sense of responsibility for household orderliness and an interest in her own "cave." By the acquisition of this defensive block, she can protect and sustain that emotional maturity she had already attained up until the point of exposure to a crippling force.

The age of three years is marked by the transition from an infantile total laissez-faire attitude to the beginning of a sense of responsibility, which includes the upkeep of her surroundings. With consistent criticism and rejection during the first thirty-six months of life, we can produce the sense of crippling shame in an infant for being a flawed, inadequate individual. In contrast, we have to be at least three years old before we can be inflicted with a sense of guilt for doing a wrong act. The sense of a conscience is normally acquired at about the age of three years.

The history of her family sheds light on the formation of this limited personality arrest during infancy. As a baby, she was cared for by her mother and later, by her grandmother. These two women had common characteristics and similar behavior traits. They are both very bright, quick thinking, decisive, and impatient. Their attitudes were that any delay on the part of another person carrying out direct or implied requests or instructions was unacceptable. Slight hesitation or slowness on the part of another would cause them to go ahead and complete the required task themselves, rather than waste time with a slow or bumbling helper.

Jill, by nature, is creative, with some artistic talent. She has taught herself to play the piano and clarinet, played violin in the school orchestra, and is a whiz in mathematics and computers. She is also highly intuitive.

In infancy, she displayed her eagerness to explore, create, and attempt maneuvers almost as soon as she began to crawl. Her mother, rather than providing a safe place and supporting her in her early attempts to be herself, put Jill aside, because she was in the way with her bumbling slowness. Mother's shunning made Jill feel ashamed of her mettlesome attempts, and, consequently, she suspended all of her efforts to make investigation, trial arrangements, and creations in her small environment.

Later in Jill's infancy, her mother and grandmother were very impatient with her "not doing things right." Jill reacted time and time again with feelings of rejection. Repeated failures in every aspect of housekeeping caused her to develop a sense of crippling shame for being a flawed and inadequate person. Her protective emotional bulkhead formed in infancy and childhood, insulating her repeatedly from probable failures. Jill learned not to let her natural drives, with those unwanted attributes, show; as a consequence she converted these outgoing traits for household activities into a state of contrite submission. This is crippling shame. With her own protective suppression, Jill kept out of the way of her mother's busy schedule. Mother did approve of most of her other behavior traits. Later Grandmother continued and intensified the stimuli for Jill to stay out of the way. For her first three years, Jill's contrite behavior, arising from feelings of being flawed, protected her from criticism and rejection for her bumbling and slowness at doing household tasks.

Any behavioral device that has protected us for years cannot be wished away. This is especially true if, at its inception, it was introduced and repeatedly reinforced with the use of anger to inflict fear. The adoption of crippling shame was the device that Jill needed to protect her soul, her self-image.

The personality arrest of crippling shame serves both good and bad. It should be only a temporary emotional bulkhead. First and foremost, it protects all the maturity in that stream of emotions that Jill had gained up to this crisis point in her life, but also, it arrests any further development in that same steam. The evidence here is that she is free and uninhibited to behave as an infant without responsibility for household chores and orderliness. We cannot manipulate her into a sense of guilt to renounce her slovenliness for that additional part of her emotional stream has never matured to the age of three, the age of responsibility. This dynamic is also operating in those individuals who routinely trash their government provided housing.

Remedial removal of this protective bulwark can

only be accomplished when Jill feels safe enough to upgrade her perception of herself. A change in her self-image can be accomplished only by her willingness to survey and accept valid additional information about herself and her separate individuality. All beliefs or changes in beliefs are entirely based on the information that is available. An infant gets stimuli from her seven senses, but has no critical judgment to evaluate this information.

As an infant, Jill formed defenses that are entirely reactive. Family circumstance forced her to adopt attitudes about herself that are a direct transfer from her caretakers. The prescription for revision of attitude is to therapeutically create a safe place, wherein Jill can broaden and accept her perception of the circumstances, environment, and her presumed inadequacy. She needs to reactivate that ancient inscribing process that is still in her subconscious mind, preferably with full emotional reexperience.

Jill has the same problem as the rest of us; subconsciously, she retains active imagery of every emotional trauma. With guidance to help her stay focused, she can simultaneously retain her current active consciousness and reenact the original scenes, and the attitudes of her caretakers, at the time of her assumption of the protective bulkhead. With an additional twenty years of intelligent understanding available to her now, she can mentally take this knowledge back to the original scene and revise it in an age reenactment session.

In therapy, Jill can use all of her current realizations about herself, her personal attributes, her years of experience, and information about people. Then, with aid of a qualified guide, who can conduct her in age reenactment, she can simultaneously entertain two perspectives. She can review all of the retained, detailed information that is so strongly embedded in her subconscious mind and match it up with her current adult appraisal. When she adds her current information, especially about her caretakers, to her original belief about her self-worth, her self-esteem, and her self-imposed place in the pecking order of human relationships, her attitudes will either be strengthened as they are, or more likely, will be adjusted. When she has both the infantile emotional event and her adult information in juxtaposition, she will, with this broadened discovery, automatically form a new perception of herself as a worthwhile person.

At present, her attitude is causing her to behave as if she is totally inadequate to do housekeeping, and her consequent fear keeps her from taking any action that might bring about a change. No amount of logical suggesting or demanding will alter her feeling about herself. Only the resumption of her interrupted and stalled state of normal evolution toward full emotional adulthood will cause her to feel differently about herself. Any lasting advance of her maturity must absolutely include two changes. First, she truthfully adjusts her beliefs about herself by enlarging her perception of the past. Second, she adjusts her attitude and expectation for the future. Her problem was installed in infancy, and only upgrading her belief about herself as she directly feels it can effect a permanent fix.

Jill adopted her belief about her inadequacy based solely on the information that was available to her during the first year of her life. Also, at that time, she was entirely limited by her immature brain and its inability to receive and process complex data concerning her parents and their emotional states and motives. Basically, she had only her seven senses— sight, sound, touch, taste, smell, intuition, and attitude perception—upon which data she was forced to assume a protective action. The two most important of these seven senses, in infancy, were her intuition and attitude perception. Although she could not make informed, logical judgments, she did, intuitively, and in self-protection, fix an assessment of her caretakers' attitudes, which she assumed directly as her own appraisal of her self-worth. She perceived that something was wrong with her, that something was unacceptable, and consequently, in defense, she had to keep this something from showing. She did convert her assertive responses to crippling shame, and was, thereby, temporarily "saved."

The revamping of her beliefs can be done only when she is able to understand—intellectually and emotionally—that the foundation of her beliefs was flawed, solely by her infantile limitations and her ability to react only to that information available to her. Now she is aware that this was incomplete information. Without any comprehension of consequences, she was able, with her limited ability, to save her life by compromising part of her individuality and assuming the wrapper of shame. This perverted self-assessment served her well, and protected her all through her infancy from losing any of her previous gains.

Look at the evidence—Jill is a bright, attractive woman with a good brain and great creativity. You know, from her present state, that she had all of these attributes when she was born. She certainly did not come into this world feeling inadequate—this was taught to her. Her belief about herself and her inability to create an orderly household was based on incomplete data.

The task is to have her apply her twenty-two years of accumulated knowledge and experience, plus her adult appraisal of realistic findings concerning her mother and grandmother, to augment the information of her infancy. Finally, intellectually, she will be able to understand the dynamics of her personality arrest. With this insight, she may, with guidance and support, be willing to reexperience and emotionally reenact the trauma of her infancy. Now, with added sophistication and information about human interactions, she can apply this knowledge to the situation in her infancy, which will enable her to upgrade her logical conclusions about her worth and ability. Only when she feels differently about herself, and her confidence in her abilities improves, will today's automatic behavior be more mature.

Case History—William

William, a homeless street person, is a forty-year-old man, first seen in group session in a veterans' sheltered workshop. To retain enrollment in this group, each individual had to remain clean and sober as well as attend two Alcoholics Anonymous meetings weekly. William's main addiction was the drug methamphetamine, and he also used alcohol and pot.

William is a born leader and became a chief in the Mexican Mafia. In prison, as on the street, his chief objective was "to beat the system." While he was incarcerated, he was a true wheeler-dealer, inventing many schemes and playing daring control games with both staff and fellow inmates. He was married to a very bright, but angry woman, and he took delight in manipulating her in her anger. After some time in criminal pursuits, he decided that life was not satisfying. He consequently enrolled in AA and a Veterans' Rehabilitation program.

When he first started with our group, he was boastful of his past exploits and was proud of how he had manipulated people and of how he had cleverly beaten the system. When reminiscing about his childhood, he painted a picture of his idealistic, large, rural, Mormon family, in which he was the youngest child. He demonstrated with ease his knowledge of the Bible by quoting numerous passages. He stated that, as he was growing up, his father, mother, and older siblings were all supportive of him. However, at the age of twenty, he became uncomfortable at home and struck off on his own. He was able to get jobs easily, learned quickly, and rose to a responsible management level routinely.

William has a gift, by which he is able to readily and accurately read peoples' emotions and understand their wants, which enabled him to be a first class con artist.

In group therapy, when allowed and encouraged, he defended a picture of his model family and their adherence to Mormon principles. He consistently assured us that during his early infancy and childhood, his home life was "as good as they come." Only gradually was he able to see and accept that there were real problems in his early childhood, and that he had formed a distorted self-image. Gradually, he began to understand how he formed his beliefs and attitudes about himself and others.

On the surface, there was a total disparity between his description of his apparent ideal rearing in his childhood and his resultant adult behavior. As an adult, he has been behaving consistently in a manner that demonstrated that he felt that he was personally unworthy. This was mystifying until we could induce him to begin to identify that his attitude about his identity was the determining force that drove his behavior. He excelled in one-upmanship and took much pride in this accomplishment. The rewards from this attitude are ethereal, for boosts from individual episodes soon wear off much like the high from amphetamine.

Competition for competition's sake alone is founded on a power struggle. Ironically, it puts the other fellow in charge, for he can keep egging us on as long as he chooses—we are committed to respond. In order to be emotionally fulfilled in this life, we need to be our own selves, by concentrating our energy on developing our particular talents that are encoded in our genes. Comparison with any other person or role model has no place when our only goal is to fulfill our own template that is in our personal genome.

When we analyze William's' infancy, we find that it was far from OK. To this day, he is so fearful that he is unable to identify his own feelings. When we reconstruct his early infancy, we find that the salient part was his super alertness and intuition, which was partially his undoing. From day one, his whole family of seven worked in concert to mold this youngest member of the family into what, in their minds, an ideal person was supposed to be. Nobody really tuned into his emotions or his needs for separateness, early exploration, and self-determination. Consequently, his perception was that he was unacceptable and rejected. Very early on, he got the message that by forsaking his identity and compromising his soul, the family would let him live as long as he followed their lead in game playing. As a consequence of this rejection, he learned to suppress his feelings and even denied to himself they even existed. His family did not accept him as he was, but rather, they did afford him immense approval for his being able to read their emotions and adjust his behavior to accommodate their wishes and directions. He steadfastly and continuously suppresses and is unable to identify his own emotions and feelings. In later infancy and childhood, he accomplished feats and tasks that were amusing and amazing for his age. Consequently, with lifelong practice from infancy, he is able to expertly identify feelings in everyone but himself, because they are important and he is not. This is the specification for a con man. Using this innate ability to read emotions and attitudes in other people became the fulfilling part of his life. This ability afforded William information to be in a position to placate and manipulate all others. He hides his feeling from everyone, even himself, because his attitude is that he is worthless.

In a sense, William has resented and despised other people's feelings—he thinks they are weak and exposed. It has made good sense for him to use and exploit these weaknesses in others. This has been his life's fascinating game. However, he has never been able to believe in his own superiority. The lack of fulfillment in his self-worth is based on his inability to fundamentally accept himself for who he truly is. His basic attitude of worthlessness about himself causes him to continuously live out this feeling.

If we had lovely young daughters, would we accept and esteem them for who they are? How much would we encourage them to be all they could be? In contrast, if we had a beaten-up, twenty-year-old car that barely ran, how much care and energy would we lavish on this vehicle? Realistically, in this life, we do only what is important to us. If our behavior invariably puts us in unenviable situations with society and the law, we need to consider who is totally responsible for getting us into these situations.

After we wrote up this case history, we had William review it to make necessary adjustments. These revisions were very few and minor. Then, in his last group session, before he moved to another city to take a responsible job, we did an age reenactment session with him. A whole multitude of defenses came to light, and all of these were designed to keep his inner feelings from showing, which in turn, helped him avoid saying anything that might display openness. He strove hard to seek what he thought we wanted to hear, but in spite of that effort, he disclosed much information about his suppressed past.

He was the baby, the youngest of five boys, and his mother loved and protected him.

"I did things for my mother and my brothers didn't," he says. "They didn't like me. They called me a little fucker. They tried to choke me. I knew I was smarter than they were. I couldn't cry. Later I tried to let my brother know how I felt, and he laughed at me. Finally, I was able to beat up my brothers."

William is highly intuitive, as was his mother. His close emotional dependency on her was the cause of envy, and it was his vulnerable point that incited attacks by his jealous siblings, who felt unable to compete.

Long-term follow up wasn't possible, but key to his recovery is that he is able to see and to change his attitude about himself. His perception of his self-worth will change as he brings into focus the true dynamics of his family's attitudes about him in his infancy. Intellectually, he is aware that he must allow himself to become a separate individual in order to fulfill his genetic template, with its special gifts and talents. As he does so, he will be able to increasingly divest those attitudes imposed upon him by his family. Finally, William will be able to assume his inalienable right to life, liberty, and the pursuit of fulfillment.

Fear Spoils the Quality of Life

To enjoy the increasing fullness of life, we need ever-widening choices. Environmental conditions and physical impairments limit many possibilities, but these are not nearly as restricting as fear. For instance, if we have acute infections or chronic impairments, such as arthritis or paraplegia, we will be limited. If, in addition, we are fearful, these impediments will not only limit our physical participation in activities, but also demand much more significantly an imposed constant drain on our very finite emotional energy. Fear stems from an attitude of being inadequate to contend with alleged challenges. Fear robs us of our confidence, which in turn imposes stifling limits on our choices. Even apprehension can dissipate emotional energy. When we dedicate emotions to make the past different, or when we fear the future, we fritter away some of our awareness of what is occurring now and limit our ability to live in the present.

Reality exists only in the present. To be in the present, we take all emotions out of the past and remove all fear of the future. To take full advantage of this moment, we need all of our discretionary energy to create current, harmonious, social interactions and joy, to be entirely our own persons, free of pretense, anger, resentment, and fear.

By subconscious choice, we elect what portion of our daily, finite, emotional energy we care to invest in self-selected entitlements. To create the most rewarding and fulfilling lives, we need to reverse the practice of squandering our emotional energy.

Because of some feeling of inadequacy we had in the past, we willfully direct and assign some or much of our energies to the constant tasks of wanting the past to be different, and to supporting fears of future events. After satisfying these entitlements, the residual portion of our emotional energy is what remains for elective choices. We need emotional energy to have interactive, social communications with those individuals that are near and dear to us. After using energy for routine daily maintenance and self-imposed entitlements, we have only a small portion of our discretionary emotional energy left to define our quality of life. To become fully mature, we must free up emotional energy that we have formerly dedicated to the past and future.

It is only wishful fantasy that we can go back and nullify the record and the dynamics of any past event or change the actions of other people by attempting to rework history to our advantage. Also, as for the future, it is folly to adopt fear which, in its very creation, implies vain hope and belief that this assumption of fear will in some way protect us from exposure to possible forthcoming unpleasant or threatening events. The exceptional person is the individual who is the most evolved or has become one with the Buddha. He has done so by freeing himself of all unrealistic attempts to change the past and has expunged fear of the future.

The past can never be changed. To keep from inadvertently repeating history, we bring to our conscious minds as many details of past events as possible, while at the same time removing all emotions from them. History is neither good nor bad—it just is. The only critical and essential change we need to make is to revise our perceptions about ourselves and our relative importance in the dynamics of the formation of our defenses. With a thorough realization of all the factors involved in past events, we can understand the now needless defenses we acquired initially. As adults, we have much more advanced brain functioning than we did during our formative infancy and childhood and can, if we are willing, upgrade our self-images. This means that we can change our perceptions of ourselves to make them conform to our personal templates as recorded in our DNA.

When we gain a thorough understanding of the possible dangers of upcoming events and evaluate the possible benefits, then we can choose to accept the risks. At that point, we can become either prepared or fatalistic, and, either way, we can eliminate fear of the future. Without fear, we can also be in charge of all our mental faculties to best contend with all exigencies. Right now, the only sure way to avoid risk in life is to drop dead. By nature, frailty of human tissue makes living a hazardous condition, and a rewarding adventure. Nothing is guaranteed. The only true security is our faith that we can contend with future challenges as they arise. We gather all the information that is available, and at the same time make contingent preparedness plans to respect dangers. With knowledgeable preparedness, we can successfully cope with those hazards. Further, we construct contingency plans, like fire drills, designed around several avoidance techniques, which, when necessary, we can act upon quickly to contend with future dangers. With well thought out plans of avoidance, we can act immediately, without our minds being clouded by high emotions.

Having made those plans, we stop worrying, trusting that we will cope with events when needed. This enables us to live in the present, with all our resources freed up and available for use now.

Green-Spotted
Yellow-Bellied Alligator

Worldwide, the attitude of anger is the most prevalent condition limiting our choices for individual development and our attainment of desirable human interactions. Anger is always about the past, even if it seems to be an effect of current situations. The past can never be changed; only our personal perceptions of the past can be revised.

Anger and aggression, like sexual drive, are vital primitive drives to sustain and perpetuate basic life forms. Anger is our ultimate reserve to keep us alive as we face imminent danger. Basic to all animals are raw aggression and anger, which are the ultimate life saving forces. When, in order to survive, we need a total body response in microseconds, the automatic activation of aggression and anger will give us our optimum chance to fight for survival. Activated anger turns on our total bodies' systems and thereby mobilizes us for life and death struggles.

When anger and aggression are unrestrained, no other persons or things matter; there is no morality or conscience in our primitive actions for survival. When we are truly threatened, active anger is our built-in, ultimate, automatic reaction. How quickly and ardently anger is activated will be determined by our own perceived vulnerability. Our responses can be partial, selectively abortive, or can crescendo. Two variables, predicted by our intuitive perception, are our self-perceived vulnerability, and our instant intuitive appraisal of the magnitude of the threat. No time is available for logic and reason.

In addition to the immediate, life-saving function of anger, there are a few limited, laudable uses of anger in every day social interactions. These secondary uses of anger are like open fire, in that they need to be strictly limited and controlled. An unsupervised and uncontrolled open fire will destroy more than we mean to burn; anger, like a wood fire, has hot embers, which consume lots of fuel and take a long time to cool down.

Seldom, in day to day life, does a person really need to activate his whole body's total response to save his life. However, the more insecure a person feels, the more often he will rely on his total reserve to repel even a slight, casual incursion of his space or demeaning of his identity. With a basic attitude of anger, the individual is always on "red alert." He invests a great share of his life's energy in readied offense, rather than defense, to retain, or gain, control and respect. With his immense insecurity, he is a predictable disaster in interpersonal relationships, because he has the expectation that every other person should conform to his wishes.

The angry person has a short fuse; that is, this immensely insecure person is the one who has innumerable publicly accessible anger-buttons. He is like a yellow-bellied alligator with green spots, and each and every spot is a turn-on switch. Let's say this ferocious, insecure, angry gator has one hundred and fifteen (last count) "green-spot-buttons." If we touch any one of these buttons, the beast can snap off our hands at the wrists or swipe us with his tail. Every one of these anger-activating buttons is available for "public access," and each is as sensitive as a hair trigger. Push one and see the animal go.

When this highly insecure alligator is swimming in the brackish water of his swamp, he may accidentally brush up against a root of a cypress tree and activate one of his own buttons. His clumsiness will excite anger, even against himself. Basically, he does not like himself for who he is. If we think his anger is directed only at us, we miss the point—he is also terribly hard on himself.

This alligator, deep within his habitat, with its weeds, algae, and muck, considers himself to be very "macho," because he gets respect from all the frogs, fish, and possums. When this animal remains in his slimy pool, his choice of activities and association with other animals is limited. When, however, he hauls himself up on the bank, he opens his vulnerability to a whole new range of possible exposures. In the bright sunlight, he exposes all of his turn-on switches to all creatures, including men, women, and children. Once he pulls himself out of protective waters and strays away from the swamp, anyone and everyone can control him. While staying clear of his teeth and tail, we may push his buttons with impunity. Without cognitive reflection, he will, in anger, automatically act out his demand for respect, and can be tormented to exhaustion at any time.

While this alligator is sustaining his offensive attitude to keep everyone from getting close to him, he is, at the same time, turning all of his emotional energy against his own body, which phenomenon, when prolonged, becomes self-destructive. Any organized group could systematically torment him to death. Such torment could be initiated by the childish taunt, "You're a yellow-bellied green-spotted reptile." Of course, such words have no power at all, unless the alligator's self-image is so insignificant that he puts power into empty words. By his choice, he creates and sustains a special public-use button for those words. Button pushing is now considered inappropriate when performed in identifiable groups, since our society, in its concern for political correctness, is returning to the attitude of the Dark Ages, when speaking derogatorily about the king could get one's head chopped off.

A constant overstimulation of active readiness of all the body's offenses and defenses will wear out the alligator's body, until one system after another prematurely malfunctions.

As awesome and macho as this beast pretends to be, in reality, he is just an out-of-control show-off. Even his one-month-old daughter can push his buttons, merely with her presence in her soiled diaper.

As a birthright, deep inside this alligator is the yearning for acceptance, closeness, and intimacy. In his first year, his parents demonstrated the attitude that he is flawed, inadequate, and unacceptable. This toxic attitude is the base cause of his over-active offensive and defensive actions. In compensation, today, he demands, for reassuring support, that his wife and daughter fill his dependency needs. Instead of according his family mutual acceptance and esteem, he demands respect, for that is all he feels he deserves. Each day, he gets even farther away from obtaining acceptance from his wife and daughter. Family members are in fearful dread that any attempt at closeness on their parts might push the alligator's buttons.

The alligator's base problem is his feeling of vulnerability that he has retained since his early infancy, when his original dependency needs were not satisfied. In reality, he is still emotionally functioning as a needy infant. Therefore, for his life's sake, he reasonably demands that when consideration is accorded to any person, he must come first. With his display of anger in his victim status, he demonstrates that the only way he knows to get respect from everyone is to demand that they pay attention to and take care of him. The object of his anger is to satisfy his powerful dependency needs.

We can understand the behavior of the intensely jealous husband, who stalks and kills his divorcing wife, when we know the beliefs and age-related attitude of this childish husband. When we gather thorough information of the history of the man's past behavior patterns, we usually find many instances of his extreme vulnerability, that is, anger. The last part of this history will have this likely scenario: His wife had been attending to and servicing this man's every unsatisfied, infantile, dependency need. This cooperative arrangement gave the appearance of a compatible marriage. Now that she has begun to feel slightly better about herself, she upgrades her expectations of him. She fantasizes in her expectations that her husband's attitude and behavior would mature at least as much as that of their developing children. She would have been satisfied with this small improvement in the level of his childish attitude and behavior. Unfortunately, he has not changed. But she has grown emotionally, and she created the problem when she stopped servicing him as if he were an emotionally dependent infant. He will do everything to restore his former position, or if necessary, eliminate her, so no one else will have that coveted serviced position. "No one else is going to have my mama!" is jealousy in the extreme.

No one, by servicing the man with his primitive attitude, can possibly satisfy him for more than a short time. The problem is his attitude, which only he can change. Attitude determines behavior. In courtship, he forced himself to temporarily adopt a more adult attitude. For a while, he could behave as an adult, but with any threatening stress or impairment with alcohol, his attitude would revert back to the earliest stage at which his emotional development was arrested. He, like the alligator, has a huge number of green spots, or public-access buttons, each of which represents an age-related attitude and a composite of beliefs of inadequacy, that, when stimulated, will set off offensive or defensive reactions.

The lifelong job of this alligator is to teach everyone in this world to treat him with respect. He has become an active member in the National Association for the Advancement of Green-Spotted Yellow-Bellied Reptiles, whose avowed goal is to teach the whole world not to dare to touch "hot" buttons. The NAAGYR does not recognize that the problem belongs to the alligators and has nothing to do with the public. The gator demonstrates individual prowess by threatening to slash us with his tail or snap us in his jaws. This display is entirely designed to make us stay clear of his public access turn-ons. His ferocious attitude and behavior demand respect proportional to his basic insecurity.

What he has really wanted from the moment of his birth is not respect, but rather acceptance and esteem, simply for being that special individual that is inscribed in his genetic template, the DNA, which he can be. In our social hierarchy, respect is the demand to gain a place. At a terrific price, it can be bought by compromising our own souls. Respect is the consolation for an individual when he foregoes even a thought of seeking self-esteem and acceptance, because he assumes it to be out of reach. He gives up his natural drive in forsaking becoming that potential person encoded in his personal genetic template. As a consoling reaction, he becomes like the sensitized alligator in the brackish swamp, forcefully seeking respect. This general phenomenon of compromise can be considered as the root cause of monumental social dysfunction, that is, anger.

We can overcome our anger by divesting ourselves of anger buttons. There are three important steps in the process:

1) We must acknowledge that we alone have the problems. We cannot expect anyone else to change permanently for our benefit.

2) We must cease actively defending ourselves and our attitudes. There is an absolute need to change our perceptions of our self-worth. Otherwise, we cannot receive new valid information that is encoded in the templates of our personal genes. This is the information that will upgrade our beliefs about our self-worth and self-esteem.

3) We must change our attitudes about ourselves, so that we will have almost unlimited futures. When we free ourselves from the limiting baggage of past false beliefs, we will have unlimited choices, insuring our maximum quality of life.

Augmentation of Imagery

Memories are recorded in our minds as precise impressions, whose formations were stimulated by the reception of information gleaned from our seven senses—sight, sound, touch, taste, smell, intuition, and attitude. These impressions, located in our midbrains, can have both emotional and body-activating components, which can be coordinated habit performances or defense reactions. If these images relate to us as persons in our environment, or to our self-placement in the human/animal hierarchy, they are images that define our self-worth and self-esteem, and, as such, are all-important in the governing of our behavior and the determining of the quality of our emotional lives.

Historically, hypnosis has both a laudable and a jaded reputation. However, the underlying mechanism of our method of hypnosis is the study and practice of altering and revising the impressions in our subconscious minds that serve as the governing influences for our bodies' functions and activities. Our subconscious minds drive the sympathetic and parasympathetic functions of our nervous systems which smooth out and coordinate all the actions and emotions that we use every microsecond of our lives.

Our conscious minds, through the use of our neocortexes, can initiate images or actions. However, our subconscious minds are needed to coordinate and handle all the millions of intricate details and direct our energies to complete those pictures and perform the attendant actions. Humans have the most advanced brains due to highly developed neocortexes, but logic, with intellectual understanding, does not change the impressions and experiences recorded in our subconscious minds, nor will our use of logic cancel the basic drives of aggression, anger, and procreation, which are constantly active in the primitive reptilian and limbic portions of our brains. If our conscious minds were all-powerful, then, with logic, we could willfully change and upgrade our attitudes, which in turn would automatically direct us to use adult habits and behavior. But this cannot be done with our conscious minds alone. This type of change must include revision of our unconscious beliefs.

The use of our minds' higher intelligence, insight, and reasoning enables us to synthesize new concepts and innovations. However, to put ourselves into production and further solve millions and millions of minute details, we have to present rough patterns of the projects to our subconscious minds, which, in turn, instantly create working templates for the projects. This process of direction is self-hypnosis. We can change our attitudes and behaviors by upgrading the impressions and consequent beliefs that are already recorded in our subconscious minds. The art of self-hypnosis involves presenting our subconscious minds with synthetic schemes that avoid all suggestions that might excite defenses that are already conjoined with previously adopted impressions. Secure, well-adjusted children can much more readily accept new suggestions, because they have few traumatic images that have multitudinous prepared fear and defense reactions. It is not our intellects that restrict our quality of life; it is our unrealistic fears and defenses, semipermanently recorded in our subconscious minds, which severely limit us.

In the long run, when we pit our intellects against our subconscious defenses in frontal assault, our subconscious minds will always prevail, because we have stimulated and activated mandatory life-saving fears and defenses. We can temporarily enforce remedial thoughts and behaviors upon ourselves, but as soon we relax our concentration, our subconscious minds will prevail by activating our old tried and true beliefs and behaviors that have served us well or saved our lives. Nature designed us in this fashion, so that our primitive forces and learned life-saving defenses take over in all unguarded moments. It is like holding our breath in attempted suicide; we are automatically forced to breathe. Theoretically, suicide by breath holding would be possible, but our conscious minds are not equal to the basic drive for survival. Similarly, we can temporarily direct ourselves to limit our overeating, but if our overeating is a learned and practiced device to compensate for the lack of personal closeness, then this altered fulfilling drive must be satisfied whenever we sense a feeling of being unaccepted.

In successful advertising, as in hypnosis, the objective is to present a desirable image by which we stimulate the emotions. With children who have simple defense patterns, it is relatively easy to engender a new picture in them. However, to reprogram an adult who has experienced a troubled and traumatic upbringing, there are many defenses to circumvent. At the very instant that a defense or resistance is excited, he is no longer listening or buying. The picture drawn for him must avoid all established defenses. It is comparable to sailing a ship through a sea littered with icebergs and maneuvering to avoid every possible collision.

The successful strategy for therapists is to create understandable, acceptable, parallel images and scenarios—scenes where there is very little hazard. Such a model might be a mental picture of sailing in a calm sea with warm water, free of floating ice, in which all cruising is relaxed. Scenes depicted by therapists should be at least at arm's length in order to avoid resistance. To protect his status quo, the patient will resist doing what he senses is threatening to his previously formed self-image. He has had vast exposure while watching movies and television; he is a successful spectator. Also, he is experienced, at least mentally, in telling other people how to better run their lives. Now, it is time to set the stage and write the scripts for clones with precisely the same attitudes as his.

Here is the gigantic problem we must face: All emotional adjustment problems we have are our own. We are the only ones who have the answers and the responsibility for their resolution. We must not think that any other person can or will change simply for our benefit. Hopefully, when we stop harassing others, they will relax and create safe places for us to grow into emotionally. The most anyone can ever do for us is to create emotionally safe places, offering helping encouragement for us to focus on our attitude adjustments and our self-worth and self-appraisals.

When the patient can visualize the idealized person or child that represents himself and consider that this clone is to be the most important individual in his life, then he can work with this image. One must be clear here to differentiate being from doing. Doing things my way is a two-year-old's attitude. By using his most vivid imagery, we can help a person shelter and direct his self-apparition out of harm's way. In his first two years of his life, his parents made him conform to the picture of the infant they wanted. With the concept of being in a safe place, he can now fantasize a clone of this esteemed little person that he used to be and watch him overcome the difficulties that he endured, or crumpled under, in his childhood. We can help him to intelligently depict his clone, protect his clone from harm, and induce him to overcome those threatening situations.

When the patient is dealing ardently in the management of his clone, he is readjusting his own subconscious impressions and beliefs about himself. By his own effort and with his own solution, he is accepting a revised attitude about his self-worth. Also, when he accepts that his clone is worthy, he simultaneously changes his basic subconscious attitude about himself.

One of the defenses most harmful to interpersonal relationships is the use of argumentation. This is an age-related attitude of someone stuck at a four-year-old level. When we desire adult interpersonal interactions, it is hard to live with an emotional four-year-old. The automatic need to blindly defend any belief rightly belongs in the sandbox on the playground.

All of our dogmas are founded on limited information, that is, the information that was available to us at the time of those beliefs' formation. We will never know everything about anything; therefore, our beliefs will be established on incomplete data. Further, our beliefs will be age-related to the instants of their inception, becoming part of our self-images and part of our personal realities, and furthermore, they will have age-related attitudes. If we remain closed minded in any area of our personalities, we will stop maturing, blocking out any consideration or reception of new valid information. Often, exposure to experience and new valid knowledge will confirm our original opinions. As we thoughtfully corroborate data, the assumption of new propositions will either constantly upgrade or reinforce our old beliefs.

With receptive listening, discussion, and disputation, we can again accept new valid information, which may reinforce our original beliefs, but will more likely modify them. With a new broader base of information, our age-related attitudes will become more mature.

Huge problems arise because most of our fundamental beliefs about our self-worth and self-esteem are routinely adopted during the first three years of our lives. That is, we form impressions of our self-worth before our brains are evolved enough to discern the consequences of what notions we accept as truth.

A normal three-year-old has a functioning midbrain, but not much discretionary power. Only later, will he develop a fully functioning neocortex. The three-year-old thinks in terms of absolutes, such as, there is only one meaning for a single word. When we are emotionally assaulted at this stage in our lives, we form defenses to protect that portion of our self-images we have already formed. In doing so, we can be emotionally arrested and forever have a three-year-old attitude. We believe there is only one answer or one way of behaving rightly. We are consequently compelled to defend most all of our beliefs in argument. Argumentation is purely a power struggle to force our usually ill-formed dogma onto someone else.

Whether working with ourselves, friends, or therapists, our job is to consider new valid information as images, which are the communication language of our subconscious minds, and which skirt around defenses that are already in the subconscious. The instant any resistance, or defense is aroused, then all new data will be rejected.

There is a mythical animal that can be associated with argumentation. This is a fire-breathing dragon with a skin that is smooth, but flawed by hundreds of raw, sensitive spots. Each of these chronic lesions represents an active dogma irritation that, when stimulated, instantly activates this dragon to snort fire to singe and disable anyone who would be so bold as to question one of his beliefs. On this immature animal, each blemish is an active part of the dragon's personality. We, as intruders, should learn that these lesions are fixed and will be defended for life's sake. This dragon is a victim of himself; therefore, it is imperative that we resist tormenting or aggravating him.

Often throughout the day, this dragon will meet another emotional three-year-old, and the two reptiles will battle, spitting fire at one another, until one acquiesces. Then, both mythical beasts can slink off to make sure that their lesions, which are deeper, are still safely in place.

In medicine, when a patient has an indolent open skin lesion, like a pressure ulcer as occurs in a paraplegic victim who may have been in one position too long, healing is difficult. Closure of the sore is more likely to take place when the plastic surgeon debrides the wound and applies a skin graft. Similarly, a patient must desire emotional growth to divest himself of exceedingly sensitive spots. An aid to such healing (therapy) is like the plastic surgeon who starts by making the ulcer base receptive (open mind) to new skin transplant (new relevant valid information).

Remaking Infantile Attitudes

We are born with attitudes that will support our survival, both physically and emotionally. As infants, our attitudes are that we are important only to ourselves. We have inborn emotional drives and attitudes directing us to mature by gaining and sustaining ourselves as separate individuals with unmistakable self-identities. In our first three years, while holding onto our separate identities, we normally transition from this entirely infantile egocentric status to that of being cognizant, responsive, and responsible to our families and groups. The importance of this transition can hardly be overemphasized, for it is the basis of the personal formation of our identities or lack thereof. The job of our parents is to support and maintain our independent attitudes, encouraging us to retain belief in ourselves.

All our beliefs are founded on information available to us at the time of their formation. Attitude adjustments will happen in us only if we accept additional information. When we form our self-images, including the feelings and images of being timid, undeserving, inadequate, or flawed, our attitudes about ourselves will be doubtful and insecure. Being equal humans does not mean that our potential talents or physical make-ups will allow us to do everything that is humanly possible, but all of us have more potential than we will ever develop. Inevitability, getting limited approval from others will curtail what we can do, but actually, we are the only ones who can keep us from being the persons we are preordained to be. Our parents may unwittingly stunt our early emotional growth, but is possible to overcome these impediments. The goal is to accept ourselves for who we are. The problem is not the acceptance of false gods, but the acceptance of flawed images of ourselves, whose traits and personae were described and mandated for us by our caretakers.

Beliefs can be revised only if we accept additional, valid information. Before remodeling can take place, we need to be aware that, regardless of anything that happened in the past, our problems now are entirely ours, alone. Dead or alive, no one else is involved in our current attitudes. In therapy, we introduce new valid, factual data to those parts of our minds that are still entirely functioning in infantile or childish modes. The information accumulated by our adult minds will be presented to those developmentally frozen, immature parts of our minds. We know in advance that these insights will be at odds with the limited data that we were able to appreciate at the time of the adoption our original self-images, when we had only infantile mental and emotional capabilities. The challenge is to get additional data past our defenses without exciting resistance. We will need to present this valid information in an understandable form in order for it to be accepted by the parts of our minds that are frozen in the past. Because parts of our minds are fixed emotionally in the past, adult logic and explanations will not register. Words are not the communication medium for young infants. Rather, we communicate with infants entirely through the exchange and interaction of physical senses, imagery, intuition, and attitudes.

Currently, we have a large, accumulated, factual

library of adult experiences and information about human behaviors, especially those of our families. Our parents' emotional problems were never our own. Many, perhaps most, of their attitudes were transferred intact from their parents. Their behavior was due to their own self-images. Our parents' behaviors and attitudes toward us were mainly for their own benefit. This was especially true if they considered us as part of them, or if they regarded us as their property—"My child." The reconsideration of all this data will revise the inaccurate or inadequate perceptions of the details of the original sensitizing events.

As normal infants, we use all of our seven senses to keep us in touch and interacting with our environment. However, the degree to which infants interact with each stimulus from the seven senses differs widely from that of adults. For example, our reactions to hunger and physical discomfort are acute. Because of only limited experience in the womb, our reactions after birth are guided very heavily by our intuition, as it is tuned into our survival drive—the survival drive entrenched in the total genetic experience of our progenitors. We project our attitudes very strongly. Our infant language of communication with our caretakers involves reception and interaction with attitudes and relies on intuitive understanding of those attitudes.

The foul-up in our early months and years was that we and our parents were on different pages of communication. Our attitudinal demands were that we must be recognized and treated as individuals who want our dependency needs fulfilled. Our caretakers wanted to shape us up to be what, in their own minds, would be the children they wanted—models of their idealized infant—likely, very subservient individuals. That is, their children would live with them with the least inconvenience.

As infants, we communicate in impressions and imagery. By re-parenting from the beginning and by carefully avoiding the stirring up of defensive responses, we can create a revised perspective of caretakers who intuitively tuned into us and supported us in all of our attempts to maintain our status as separate and equal individuals.

As infants, we could not describe or explain what was taking place during emotional assaults as we developed our protective emotional bulkheads. However, we recorded, in our subconscious minds, a complete set of exact impressions of those sensitizing incidents, with all their details of circumstance, sight, sound, and fury. These scenes can be revisited and reactivated exactly as if there were happening for the first time. Today, during reenactment sessions, where we can be in two time frames simultaneously, we can transfer back our current valid information and adult understanding to the original childhood scenes. Our adult minds have acquired information about people and normal human behavior and, more especially, profiles of our parents' standard reactions. These give perspectives that allow us to reinterpret those emotional events recorded in our subconscious minds in childhood.

We can readily be in two states of mind at one time. It is similar to being in a theater with very riveting action taking place on the stage or screen; emotionally we are very engrossed in the action, but we are still aware that we are in a theater. In active age-reenactment, first, we are aware of being adults, and second, we experience ourselves as troubled infants. When we add this new valid information to our original perceptions of the initial incidents, our attitudes are reframed with entirely new and revised insights. With this added information, we come away drawing obvious conclusions and revising our beliefs about relationships between ourselves and our caretakers. But more importantly, we gain added insights into our own genetic blueprints.

In treatment using active imagery, an effort is made to depict the individual at his start, when his emotions were entirely intact, and he was still as he came into this world—his own person. When his family fails to acknowledge that he is a separate and equal individual, he has to compromise part of his being (soul) to accommodate his caretakers. To save his skin, he will, to a greater or lesser extent, take on the persona they want him to take. Play-acting at being this altered emotional self is a curse that he has been required to endure all his life.

The remedial treatment of damaged self-image has two parts. The first is to get an adult understanding of how the low self-image was formed. The second, and far more important and more difficult part, is to present this information to that infantile or childish part of the mind in an acceptable form. It is difficult for any person to release attitudes and behaviors that, since birth, have been protective life-saving defenses, which have worked unfailingly throughout the years. Solely working with the conscious mind will not remove them. We need to return to the onset of their origin and adjust the infantile and childish attitudes by having the immature part of the mind accept new valid data.

It is absolutely essential to avoid any hint of frontal confrontation that would activate a defense. The patient needs to feel that he is in a completely safe place. An intellectual understanding of the problem and its origin helps a great deal. There is no value in starting therapy, unless the patient accepts total responsibility for his problem. If he will not acknowledge that the cause of his problem is a miscommunication, then we are working with the wrong person. We might ask him to identify that person or those other people whom he thinks must change for his benefit. Eventually, he will realize that no one else can ever solve his emotional problem, and he is not ready for effective therapy until he accepts this.

The technique of imagery is based on the ability to communicate with a partially matured mind that is transfixed at an immature emotional level. In order to be understandable and receptive, we must revert back to language or a mode of communicating that is understandable and non-threatening.

A guide can get most adults to use their minds to compose imagery that tunes into some or all of the seven senses, stimulating them with acceptable, fixed impressions. It is a little easier if the patient has had extensive hands-on dealings with small children, but every one has had personal experience through his own stages of growth. The basic theme consists of the exercise and practice of re-parenting the emotionally arrested infant that rules within the dysfunctional person. A fundamental assumption is that the patient has within him that undeveloped potential to become a fully emotionally developed person. Working with imagery of idealized parents who are able to communicate as equals with the child, the infant is at last able to expand into the template potential of his genetic encoding.

It is essential at the outset that we accept that this emotionally intact infant did exist. Next, we need to create the scenes and circumstances wherein we can imagine receptive, understanding parents. It is essential that these imagined caretakers project the attitude of acceptance. Their chief job is to regard their infant as a separate and equal individual. Vivid imagery projects these revised idealized parents as able and willing to touch and hold the baby, all the while emanating an attitude that they are totally involved with what they are doing. Their gentle supporting touch conveys that they have esteem for and acceptance of the baby. Their warmth and cradling of the infant is reminiscent of the security that this child had while still in the womb. When the infant is nursed and fed, he will be relaxed when his hunger is first satiated. His dependency needs get continuing gratification and reassurance with the tender holding after the feeding.

He needs to develop very few or no new defenses because his environment is almost free of the former family's continuous hostility toward one another. All expressions of anger and argumentation are gone.

The projected imagery continues as these idealized parents, from the start, steadfastly support the bumbling infant in all of his explorations and experimental attempts in his changing environment. These loving parents gently guide him away from potential hazards. Until he is almost three-years-old, the caretakers actively attempt to teach nothing, but rather only assist in what he initiates. Active instruction will start at the age of three.

The patient's problem is not poor memory; his real problem is that he remembers everything of emotional importance. In fact, the origins of his emotional problems seldom remain in his conscious memory, but each and every emotional trauma and its resultant defense is very active and alive in the archives of his subconscious mind. They are recorded there, because they are retained as subconscious defenses in the form of precise impressions of incidences. If it were not so, no individual would be afraid of the dark, have stage fright, fear women or old men, or worry. Only because of past experiences, he has been obliged to assume protective reactions and learned evasive devices. An exception is that, engraved in the brain of a newborn are those instinctive fears and survival techniques that have been passed on to him from millions of generations of his progenitors through his genes.

An illustration will help develop the point. If someone falls while skiing and breaks a leg, he will hurt for a while and be inconvenienced temporarily. But soon, he will be back on the slopes as before.

What if he suffers an "emotional broken leg," such as being stranded when small and alone, losing a loved one, getting rejected as a two-year-old who wanted to be held and loved, etc? He will subconsciously remember such incidents in full living color for the rest of his life, that is, unless he defuses the emotions of that incident before his subconscious mind converts the pain into a fear and a defense. This automatic fear and defense will guard us against experiencing that emotional loss again, but at the high cost of limiting our self expression in that area. Sooner or later, if we desire to live fully, we will have to release that defense and step boldly into our full dimensions.

Good and Evil

Good and evil evolve as diverse operating qualities of human behavior. One religious concept is that we have two angels, one sitting on each shoulder. The first angel urges us to do evil, and the second counsels us to do good. When we take an overall reality examination, we find that good and evil are derived from a common origin, which is universal, because all living creatures have the same type of genes composed of DNA.

Some scholarly people debunk evolution, but, to do so, we would have to disregard the great bulk of scientific discoveries over the last one hundred years. In the past half-century, research laboratories and pharmaceutical companies have developed and marketed dozens of antibiotics that have been clinically effective. Recently, we have seen the progressive loss of effectiveness of antibiotics, like penicillin, in their ability to prevent growth and to kill disease bacteria, such as streptococcus pneumonia, which cause sinusitis and pneumonia. At the time of their FDA approval, dozens of these antibiotics were tested and found to be very effective in the control of certain bacteria. Now, almost without exception, these bacteria and organisms have mutated in self-defense. Consequently, each antibiotic has lost a little or a great amount of efficacy. That is, in response to specific, chemical, bacterial poisons, these living microscopic creatures have developed individual, protective defenses. In spite of antibiotic use in formerly effective doses, these bacteria and fungi have regained their virility. They, as mutants of the original organisms, can again grow and destroy human tissue in the presence of the first generation of antibiotics. These lowly disease bacteria have evolved by adjusting and adapting advanced internal chemistry, which can now avoid destruction by antibiotics. This adaptation to cope with a new environment demonstrates the ability of living matter to slightly change DNA to better assure survival.

On a much larger scale, this same adoptive phenomenon has prevailed in the evolution in all living species including Homo sapiens. This evolution occurs not only in chemical metabolic reactions, but also in developing social behaviors.

All animals have evolved rules in their dependent relationships by trial and error. These slow changes by incremental adjustments have achieved adaptation for a better chance of long-term group survival. If these mutations did not happen, those static species have, with few exceptions, become extinct.

Whatever attitudes and behaviors we consider to be "evil" are no more than the normal, primitive survival techniques that are still present in the so-called lower animals. The evolving nature of RNA and DNA, essential to primeval animals as well as our ancient ancestors, is designed primarily to insure survival and procreation. These survival imperatives are not concerned about etiquette, plunder, killing, and the ignoring of another species' rights to exist. Every so-called evil was a normal life-sustaining attitude and behavior for basic life forms.

The human embryo starts out as a one-celled individual. With further growth, each embryo and fetus reenacts the progressive development through all of the physical stages and primitive anatomical forms of our ancient ancestors (ontogeny recapitulates phylogeny). Occasionally, when fetal embryonic growth is interrupted, the evolving child will retain an ancient physical part or mechanism, which we regard as a congenital abnormality. This defect is directly related to a specific time in embryonic development and results from interference in its growth. One such defect is congenital "clefts" in the neck, which represent a partial arrest in evolutionary development. It is the retention of the gills, whose formation we, as a species, needed when these gills were a necessary functioning part of our primitive ancestors who lived in the water.

Physical development and growth is more assured than developing emotional maturity. Emotional growth is much more sensitive to disease and impaired development than physical growth. In a true sense, in human behavior there is no evil, but only lack of human emotional evolution.

In science, we similarly consider "cold" to be nonexistent, that is, there is no such state. Cold is merely a feeling of comparison—cold is the absence of heat. Absolute zero (-472º Fahrenheit) is the state in which a substance has no heat. Every object in our everyday world has a degree of heat. Similarly, evil is the primitive state, wherein living creatures have not yet evolved enough intellectually and emotionally to consider the inalienable rights of other living creatures to develop in their own best forms. This becomes a bit complicated, because all life forms, except the very lowest, are sustained only by living and consuming lower life forms. This is called the food chain. Also, each species must afford some recognition and preferential treatment to its own kind.

While not infringing upon another person's individuality, being our own persons is the ultimate measure of human emotional maturity. As distinct individuals, we can best live in a society in which there is the least disruption of this special Homo sapiens' emotional behavior.

Conscience is probably only present in the more highly developed animal forms; it is especially the hallmark of human evolution. It is not present at birth in humans, but normally develops at about the age of thirty-six months, and under stress, it does not automatically develop as it should. When, in the first two years of a human being's life, his individuality is compromised, continuous emotional development is severely impeded or permanently stalled. When an individual is made fearful of allowing himself to normally assume added emotional maturation, this development does not automatically resume, even when the former threat is gone. As an infant becomes an adult and is aware of his emotional hang-ups, he must have a special degree of assurance and personal safety before he can allow his emotional development to resume in a normal manner.

The development of emotional impairment in the infant is similar to the anatomic physical abnormalities in the early human fetus. Just as in the previously mentioned birth defect, the physical out-growing of the gill clefts is disrupted, similarly, if the emotional maturation of the infant is disrupted, the child is left with the emotion responses of a more primitive human life form. This primitive form, by its evolutionary basis, has no conscience, but retains, partially or almost completely unrestrained, the normal primitive self-survival drives of lust, brutish aggression, sex, and murder.

Concern for the rights of others to coexist in evolving societies must be present in a large portion of human society to have continuous peaceful community. This can only occur when the majority of people have evolved enough emotionally to have consciences and morality. However, even the most highly emotionally advanced individuals have a little of the devil on one shoulder.

Our Continuous Conversation

We all have continuous silent conversations with ourselves, wherein we define ourselves to ourselves. This means that on a quiet, inner level that is not conscious, we are continually saying who we are. These definitions of ourselves are usually formed early in life with inadequate information, based on how we are regarded by the people around us, and the result is that most of us define ourselves in very limited ways. The harm is that we all have great potentialities that are, many times, left out of our externally derived and internally accepted definitions of ourselves, and we are, therefore, limited in the degree to which we are able to experience and express those potentials.

For example, we may define ourselves by our

work, our families, or our inner feelings, whatever they may be. For some of us, they are rich, warm, expanded feelings, but most of us feel somewhat flat and not greatly inspired throughout our days. Our feelings can be changed by expanding the content of our silent, ongoing, internal conversations. We do this by acknowledging all that we are, whenever it is apparent. For example, many of us, at certain times, have moments of great inner inspiration, when we experience love or clarity of vision. At those times, we are, indeed, noble. We can include this reality into our ongoing conversations by announcing to ourselves the truth, which is, "I am noble." When we say positive phrases like that to ourselves, or to our partners, who are undertaking the same transformations and are suitable listeners, then the descriptions begin to be included in our internal definitions of ourselves. Likewise, all of us, at times, have felt extreme joy and if, at those times, we acknowledge that, "I am a source of deep joy to myself and to others," this becomes included as well. We might also have occasion to say, "I am wise," since all of us have moments where our wisdom comes to the fore, and we recognize it as such. Simply announcing all that we are and claiming all that we are is of tremendous significance in our self-development, and these simple acts should be part of our everyday lives, expanding us to our true statures by extending the range of our own self-descriptions, which proceed continuously, and unconsciously, all day, every day, into manifestation.

The Origin of Thought

We have all surely noticed, in moments of reflection, that thought is a nearly constant experience of the conscious state. We are thinking almost all the time, and the question arises, from where does thought come? Thought doesn't seem to be under our control, and those who think they have control over their thoughts are asked to demonstrate it by not thinking for one hour while awake and conscious. Hardly anyone can stop thinking for even a moment out of sheer will. Certainly, there are meditation techniques that may reduce thought, but here, we are considering direct, conscious control over our thinking. This cannot be done. So, if we are not in control of our thoughts, then who is?

Descartes is quoted as saying, "I think, therefore, I am." However, he had it exactly backwards; in fact, merely being alive puts us in the situation of having a constant stream of thought, so, more correctly, Descartes might have said, "I am, therefore, I think." As some wag has said, it was a question of putting Descartes before the horse. In any case, thoughts are a fact of life which does not appear to be under our control.

We also notice that our actions spring from thought. First, we have thoughts, and then we manifest those thoughts as actions. The impulse to get up and turn on the TV results in reaching for the remote and pressing the button. So, if actions spring from thoughts and we do not control our thoughts, then who is in control of our lives? Some may say, "Well, I can't control whether or not I have thoughts, but I can control what I think." Oh, really? If that is the case, let us see where that thought came from. In other words, if you decide to embark on a program of positive thinking and do participate and succeed to some degree, where did the thought to embark on the program come from in the first place? The apparent control that we seem to exert at times only begs the question of the origin of the thought to wield that control in the first place. If it is argued that our thoughts are the result of our past and the interactions we have had with others, including our parents, as children, then where did that influence arise? In other words, the thoughts of our parents that motivated their behavior—where did those thoughts come from, etc.? Once again, this is just begging the question of who is in charge of the thinking process, and from where do thoughts arise?

The origin of thought is the same as the origin of all other phenomenon in nature. In other words, from where do trees arise? From where do rocks arise? From where do oceans arise? The only answer available to us is, we don't know, but they're obviously here, and so they have been created. The suggestion of creation implies a Creator; however, all agreement stops there since everyone then proceeds to depict his own personal projection of what a creator might be. Often, it is anthropomorphic in nature, and for others, it's an abstract force of evolution. In any case, we have to accept that natural phenomena, such as weather and the physical environment, occur. Among these other miracles, we should include thought as being as profound, mysterious, and entirely natural as every other phenomenon in nature, and of the same origin. This does not preclude our enjoying the appearance of free will and all of the delicious experiences that such activity may hold for us and upon which this book is based.

Our True Identity

A typical answer to the question, "How do you know you exist?" would be, "I know I exist, because I have thoughts and feelings, and when I look in the mirror, I see myself." These are all true enough, but, for each of these points, consider the question, "Is it subject or object?" Concerning the environment, it is easy to agree that the environment is an object of our awareness. We're aware of the world around us, whether it is our immediate surroundings, such as the room that we're in, or more distant surroundings such as the world outside, the planet, the stars above, the sun in the sky. And more intimate experiences, such as our own bodies—are they subjects or objects? If we think about it, we realize our bodies are also objects of awareness, regardless of how intimately we feel bodily sensations.

Our thoughts, if we consider them, also turn out to be objects. In other words, they are energies and activities of which we are aware. We are aware of our thoughts, so they are objects of our awareness. So what, then, is subject? Who is the perceiver? This is an ancient question, and the answer is, awareness itself. Awareness is something that we cannot see or feel directly. If we could feel it or see it, it would become an object of awareness rather than being the subject. So, by definition, that which we truly are can never be directly experienced. It is that by which we experience. The purpose of discussing this is to begin the self-inquiry process.

It is important to be clear on the difference between subject and object—between our true selves, which we can never see as objects, and everything else, whatever we experience. If we consider awareness, we realize that it is a unity, a singularity. It may be that at times when we are tired, what we're aware of is fatigue, a diminished perception of the environment, and less clarity of thought, but nonetheless, we are aware. Simply, the objects of awareness have changed. All the different people of the world are aware of bodies completely different from ours, as well as completely different thoughts, different family members, and different languages. What is the same is awareness. They are aware of all of those elements and objects of their experience. In the end, awareness is a single entity; there is only one awareness, and we all participate in that awareness. This is our true identity. We are awareness, or even more correctly, the beingness that is aware. Notice that awareness has no parts, no dimension, no location, and it has no features that can be observed. It, itself, is the observer. So, it turns out that we are something that cannot be located, cannot be identified by shape, size, color, form, or location, and is true for all persons. We can experience our own awareness, and in fact that awareness that we are is the same awareness with which we are reading this book. That awareness is our ultimate identify, and the ultimate reality of our lives, without which we do not exist. This fact–that we are awareness–is the reason that, regardless of our age, we always feel the same, because in fact, we are the same. It's still us. It's always us. That never changes because awareness is immutable.

Many people, in their quiet moments, search deep within themselves and experience their highest aspirations, their deepest truths, their clearest connectedness with life, and feel these are experiences of their souls. In reality, these are experiences of subtler levels of experience, subtler and more profound objects of which we can become aware. Souls, as usually described, are still objects, and are external to the deepest reality, which is the awareness of beingness.

Kim will always remember the profound words of his teacher, Damien Kirk, who said, "You're not who you think you are, Dr. Kim." At first, this seemed enigmatic, but eventually, the absolute correctness of the statement became apparent; anything we think is an object of our experience, and not the experience itself, and therefore, anything that we think we are is not who we are; by definition, it is only a thought. It turns out that the highest reality, which is our true identity, is something we can be, not something we can think.

We can think many, many thoughts and have an entire range of experiences, some divine and celestial, some mundane. However, we cannot have an objective experience of the subject, which is awareness itself. In the end, we can live reality, and we all do live reality, but we cannot think reality, because we think in words and concepts, and the ultimate reality is neither a word nor a concept. It is the direct experience of being, which we experience in the form of awareness.

The more clearly we come to understand this reality, the more independent we become of the vicissitudes of our lives. We begin to feel the underlying bliss of being and are less and less concerned with the ups and downs of our moods and the content of our feelings. Far from making us detached, this makes us more and more able to be with all of life and include and accept every aspect of ourselves and those around us.

This acceptance is love, and it is love that heals. There is a tremendous healing power released when we begin to accept the reality of our true identities, which allows us to become more and more accepting and, therefore, more and more loving. The purpose of this book is to help create this state by bringing to light the belief system that underlies our usual experiences and to show how it can be unraveled to release us from gripping beliefs that have limited us in the capacity to understand, to feel, and to express our innate potentials.

Summation: Be True to Thyself

The *Torah, Holy Bible, Book of Mormon, Koran* of Mohammed, and the *Veda* are all regarded by groups of people to be sacred, or the word of God. As far as believing about the origin of these books, we regard ourselves as agnostic. What we do believe to be self-evident is that a Supreme Force in the Universe designed and created, especially for us, a template of DNA genetic code that is in every cell of our bodies. This genetic code is the "sacred book," especially written for us. Furthermore, that creative force has given us the mandate to fulfill as much of that template's potential as we can in this lifetime. We are inherently designed to be, not only Homo sapiens, but also distinct individuals among all other humans. The major part of our genetic templates is first, to be human animals, and secondly, to be specific persons.

The late philosopher, Joseph Campbell, admonished us to, "Follow our own bliss," which means, "Be our own selves," or, "To our own selves, be true." The world will come down on us hard if we insist on simply doing our own thing, because invariably, we will be infringing upon another person. However, eventually we are the only ones who can prevent ourselves from being our own persons. Quite simply, emotional dysfunction results when, for the expediency of staying alive, we take on and play out the personae of individuals that differ from the potentials encoded in our personal genes. The personae that are alien to us are usually the only ones that are approved by our families or tribes. Early on, for our lives' sake, we must go along with someone else's program. However, eventually freeing ourselves to be our own separate and equal individuals is our lives' mission.

In medicine, the very best therapy is prevention. This dictum is especially true for the prevention of the adopting of immature attitudes, emotional disorders, and malevolent behaviors. We hope that, when we understand the principles of formation of beliefs and attitudes, we gradually let each human be his own person. The basic principle in child rearing is to respect and treat the infant as separate and equal. Following this course, in generations to come, the ultimate development will be to civilize our society.

Epilogue

When we come into this world, we are victims, because we are nearly helpless physically, intellectually, and emotionally. We are restricted because our nervous systems are yet to develop to the point where we can perceive much of this wonderful universe with all of its complexities. Later in life, with increased maturation of our brains, we can choose to use all of the tools of our minds to help study, analyze, and understand human attitudes. We can learn how beliefs and attitudes are formed and how they control behavior. The ultimate in emotional growth and maturity is to be completely accepting of ourselves and to develop as many of our inborn potentials as time allows.

The human mind has evolved through millions of

generations. With thoughtful study, we can begin to realize our unique place in the whole fabric of living creatures. The more we learn to appreciate and understand the systematic organization of human interactions, the more there is still to learn about interdependence.

However, when we direct our minds to voluntarily stop seeking and receiving new information, we lose zest for life. This can happen at any time, but especially in our dotage, for without the continuous inquiry for expansion of our understanding, we condemn ourselves to slip ever more deeply into defending a state of fixation, which includes only safe (politically correct) attitudes. Too often, aging individuals are subject to Alzheimer's disease and senile dementia, in which their attitudes and behaviors revert back to early, undeveloped states of infantile childishness. More tragically, even at a young age, we can selectively resist emotional growth by defending old, unaltered, original beliefs. The epitome of such shut downs is to limit our awareness, and thereby confine our focus, to such mundane occurrences as the wrinkles in the bed sheets, which we might perceive as prejudiced against us, personally.

During the past five millennia, we humans have made astounding progress in intellectual attainment and mechanical, structural, and electronic inventions, but in the vital area of societal attitudes, which determine interpersonal relationships, we have evolved hardly at all.

Traditionally, we honor the developers who produce the obvious tangible products, but such marvels can only exist because of the toolmakers who preceded them. These toolmakers include not only the makers of gadgetry, but public health engineers and social planners, like those who contrived the U.S. Declaration of Independence and the U.S. Constitution, who are the real benefactors of mankind. Without new and special tools, progress would stand still or even go retrograde. Our minds are our bags of tools, used to understand and construct our places in the hierarchy of human beings.

Our lifetime assignment is to use our conscious minds to voluntarily inform and train our subconscious minds. Our subconscious minds semiautomatically manage our attitudes, habit patterns, and our bodily actions and organs. We can voluntarily choose to direct our conscious minds to attempt to advance our understanding and prevent personal emotional dysfunction. We need to sharpen our wits by accepting new valid information as to how to deftly direct the continuing self-programming of our subconscious minds.

The basic functioning unit is a belief. Beliefs form attitudes. Attitudes determine basic behavior patterns. The objective is to understand how beliefs are formed and how they can be revised by adopting new, valid, insightful information.

The basic integrating faculty of the human mind is that of arbitrator for belief formation and readjustment. All beliefs are formed based on the information derived and integrated from the stimuli that we perceive through our seven senses—sight, sound, touch, taste, smell, intuition, and attitude. Attitude is pivotal, because it represents the summation and recapitulation of the impact resulting from all of our past experiences. Attitude is like sonar or radar in that it sends out a signal of who we are and what we are, as well as serving as a receiving unit intercepting the broadcasted attitudes of all of the persons and animals with whom we are currently interacting. Mutual attitudinal interactions and evaluations are the functioning stage upon which almost every human interaction is carried forward as an on-going relationship.

Attitudes are formed and adjusted by revisions in beliefs. With our present system of attitudes in place, we use our minds by choosing expectations for the future. Our attitudes, combined with our expectations, initiate our behaviors. Our emotional responses are the derivative of the results of our actions seasoned by our expectations. If our expectations are realistic, our results are satisfying and sustaining. If our expectations are unrealistic, we can set ourselves up for a host of various emotions, mostly unwanted. The basic fact of life is that we alone are responsible for our expectations, and consequently, our emotions.

Inevitably, our attitudes about our self-identities, (self-acceptance and self-esteem), create our quality of life. In our communities, the collective attitudes of individuals determine whether there is harmony, peace, or rampant dysfunction.

We, as parents, are the vital teachers for our children, because, in the first three years, and more especially in the first twelve months, we will be the modeling influences for our children's individual identities for the rest of their lives. They will instinctively adopt our senses of self-worth or lack of self-worth and self-esteem. Early infancy is the vital period, in which they adopt their basic beliefs or fail to adopt beliefs for assessing their personal worth and self-identities. We need to be aware that our beliefs about our own identities, whether expanded or limited, form our personal attitudes which are like virulent viruses that always spread to our children. Attitude and intuition are our prime communication languages during infancy.

As adults, in order to understand attitude and become teachers to our children, we should seek information ourselves. We need to be open to all types of information and reasonable experiences, for those exposures will upgrade our own evolving beliefs and consequent attitudes. When our reception for new valid information is closed, we are on the decline into old age and senility.

A good example of attitude is found in the positive and negative traits of a normal infant. The unpleasant traits of an infant are, in reality, not negative, because these are inborn, normal, survival techniques. They represent the maximum capability of the baby's defensive devices—the demand that someone satisfy the needs of an utterly helpless individual.

The severely dysfunctional adult has poorly retained or inadequately developed his normal positive traits, such as enthusiasm, warmth, and inquisitiveness. In most of us, these positive traits are insufficiently developed because, very early on, our energy was spent protecting our lives and individualities; when we were totally dependent persons, and we were forced to use continuous defensive responses. These came at the expense of compromising our individualism and integrity. Consequently, our attitudes today persist as infantile defensiveness, that is, the type that can be characterized as being of the "dark side of man." As neonates, each of us has temporarily had these attitudes after birth and in early infancy. This condition is a part of our individual, normal, emotional evolution that represents a necessary transition from the dependency state.

Adult responsibility can begin to develop only when, from birth to the age of three and beyond, we allow a child to evolve emotionally as he is inwardly directed by the blueprint which is predetermined in his individual human DNA. A skilled Japanese gardener can stunt the growth of a tree to make it a bonsai. In a like manner, an emotionally needy parent who is unskilled in parenting, can bonsai the emotional development of his child. The parent, like the bonsai gardener, has in mind how his tree should look years from now. The uninformed parent has specifications on how his infant should behave right now to fit into what he thinks an ideal baby should be, often to fit his own convenience. He is going to "shape him up" to fit his own picture of what a child should be—a picture often learned from his own parents. He misses and seriously represses the most important clues, which are coming from his baby's innermost drives.

The seriously dysfunctional people in our society, including criminals, wife beaters, career homeless, and addicts, are all victims because they have been bonsaied in their emotional development during infancy. These severely emotionally dysfunctional individuals, when stressed, operate with behaviors that are normal infantile attitudes and behaviors, and can be considered as merely acting out the traits that represent the "dark side of man." This so-called abnormal, amoral, or aberrant behavior is, in reality, merely the reenactment of normal infantile attitudes and behaviors and is anachronistic.

Society does not understand the origin or need

for prevention of these individuals' serious emotional dysfunctions, but society does begrudgingly tolerate them, and by rationalizing, gives this wretched behavior a pass. In contrast, when an infant from the very start is accepted as a separate and equal individual, his "good side" automatically and normally develops because he has outgrown the need to be resistant and obnoxiously defiant in an effort to assert his rightful personhood.

When we dampen or extinguish the expression of the laudable traits of infancy, the child may "stuff" them inwardly to keep them from showing, because the mere appearance of these traits makes the child unwanted. Throughout his life, the reactive memory of his parents' revulsion to these good, native qualities causes him to behave with an attitude of toxic shame for being a flawed person.

When we forcefully try to rid an infant or an adult of undesirable traits such as anger, rage, and personal disrespect, no matter how good our intentions, this "flawed individual" will perceive our efforts as an attack. We may think that we are doing something for a person's good, but we are only exciting and strengthening the expression of his protective defense. He developed, and still needs, this protection as an emotional bulkhead, which, in essence, is saving some small part of his initial identity. Harsh discipline and punishment primarily serve to perpetuate expression of these dark qualities. In fairness, when we find these dark qualities in the lower animals, we do not regard them as evil, for they are simple survival techniques common to all creatures. Our problem is our expectation that an apparently normal human should have matured emotionally and is responsible and considerate of others. Normal development for a child who, from the start, has been accepted as separate and equal is to grow into a human with consciousness of all others and a conscience.

To sustain mammalian life, each creature must retain his functioning reptilian brain with its attendant brutish and animalistic behavior. Reptilian attitude and behavior is designed for moment to moment survival. All of us have gone emotionally through this phase of the "dark side of man," and, hopefully, have had "safe places" to be allowed to develop way beyond this infantile phase.

Physically, we can normally outgrow some temporary bodily incapacity and ineptness, but emotionally, overcoming undesirable personality traits requires the willingness to allow ourselves to have a change in attitude about our self-images.

All of us, including emotionally mature individuals, will pretend to be adults. The difficulty and strain of prolonged pretense is proportional to the number and severity of our emotional arrests, which we have brought forward from infancy and childhood. Acting out the dark side of life is merely a reenactment of infantile behavior, which is an anachronism; it is merely a reenactment of early age-suspension in emotional growth.

Our attitudes and mind sets for the ideal parenting of our children must include adult understanding, patience, empathy, and acceptance. The highest qualification for being parents is to be totally accepting of ourselves, because in that state of mind, we will have no need to compete with our children or to force our personal attitudes on them. Our sole objective will be for them to be themselves. Any part of us that is in conflict with the template inscribed in our personal genes will consume emotional energy that we cannot exert toward the acceptance of our children. An oft quoted truism is, "If you are not for me, you are against me." This is exactly what the infant feels, as the language of an infant is the perception of mutually emanated attitudes. This is especially true when this conflict is within us. This is the base cause of most emotional problems and their resultant dysfunctional behavior.

In addition, within us, internal turmoil constantly stimulates our defenses and immune systems, which then turn against us. The phenomenon, in which our vital emotional energy is turned against ourselves, is the cause of half of all physical illness.

With true self-acceptance, we make no comparisons of ourselves with other people. Our only true gauge of emotional evolution is the acknowledgment of the degree to which we are now fulfilling the templates encoded in our personal genes. From birth onward, our physical and emotional need is to sustain or regain the self-confidence that we had as newborns, by assuming normal, human, emotional growth. We do not need to prove anything to anybody— we just are.

Freedom to do as we please is bound to incite others to attempt to impede or prevent us from infringing on their territory. Doing differs from being ourselves. Eventually, only we can limit our freedom to be and to think. When we consider that our thinking should in any way be dependent on approval of others, we have chosen to be victims. As victims, our good will always depend on what they choose to do. This is especially true when we imagine that their actions are responsible for our emotions, as in, "You make me angry," or, "The devil made me do it." As adults, we alone are responsible for our emotions. Most of the time, we create and set up the conditions or events that will ignite and stimulate our emotions. How we respond and how we feel are determined by our attitudes and expectations, that is, how realistic or unrealistic we are.

To state this principle again, we alone are responsible for our emotions. The rub is that every defensive attitude that we hold dormant has a public access handle that we offer to the world to potentially use to control us adversely. If all our attitudes about ourselves are supportive for our individuality, then the public, even in an attempt to manipulate us, can only support us for who we are. When we falsely maintain attitudes about self-alleged inadequacy, then we invite everyone with malicious intent to punch the buttons that will turn us on internally, starting predictable, practiced emotions to take control over us.

Anger is part of our offensive survival drive, and its use has very limited place in adult society. On the other hand, the attitude of anger is the epitome of personal inadequacy because the public, by pushing buttons, can easily and readily activate our infantile defenses. All those who, by accident, or with malicious intent, want to control us by pushing our buttons are free to do so. These actions alienate us in all interpersonal closeness, and also make us wantonly spend our energy, both outwardly and inwardly. When people are angry with us, we can figuratively step aside and let them pass, limiting the effect of their anger, so that it affects only them in a self-destructive, inward way. We cannot solve others' emotional problems. If we maintain vigilant, angry attitudes, we demonstrate that we do not like the awareness of our own inadequacies, and that we have little confidence in our own competency.

Except in sudden emergencies, each of us expends our emotional energy where we choose. Our degree of maturity can be graded by how discriminating we can be in using our emotional energy. The farther from reality we are in our expectations, the more we waste emotional energy. This is felt as resentment, fear, disappointment, and other unpleasant feelings.

We will achieve enlightenment and the state of being when we divest ourselves of all anger and resentment for wanting the past to be different and all fears for the future. In this unencumbered state, we can have all of our emotional energy available in the present. This is reality; it is the only true state there is. The past is lifeless history and the future is never here. Any attempted living in either of these two states is merely fabricated by our minds.

When we free our cognitive minds of emotions, then we can contemplate and consider all things. As adults, we can choose to let our contemplations stimulate emotional responses, but we are not victims of all images we conjure up.

We, alone, are responsible for our own feelings. They are ours, for we have bought into them. This is an essential part of true freedom. We are captives, not only of the people who demand compromise of our personal integrities, but more especially, of our own relinquishing of our separateness in order to placate other people. We escape our personal adverse control by remembering the past, converting all past emotional responses to history, and retaining the historic details. As we do so, we grant amnesty to ourselves and all others. We do this by emotionally outgrowing the need for defenses that we acquired in infancy and childhood. Further, we divest ourselves of all attitudes that do not conform to natural law. The goal is allow ourselves to grow emotionally, so our realistic expectations seldom cause untoward reactions.

A simple example: A small child is eating a hot dog, but sets it down momentarily, and in a flash, his pet collie wolfs it down. The child cries because he feels deprived. His father, in a fit of anger, kicks the dog. A true adult would let himself know instinctively that what happened was entirely normal. The small child heedlessly put down the bun and frank, and the dog naturally ate whatever became available. The father could choose to use his intellect, or he could fall back to infantile behavior in an angry attempt to punish the dog.

Every minute, each person (and animal) has an attitude. It is the gross clue about where he is coming from; his history and past experiences cause him to have a feeling about his self-image. From his demeanor and behavior, we increasingly understand where a person is coming from and at what levels he has personality arrests. From age-relating his attitude, many of his reactions are predictable. We practice routine analysis of attitude until it becomes an automatic habit. This practice will not only openly increase our understanding, but will also keep us from being judgmental.

Appendices

---

a. The Technique of Directed Age Reenactment

NOTE: This is the method Ted uses in conducting age reenactment sessions. Directed age reenactment is not a do-it-yourself technique, but a powerful therapeutic tool for use by trained professionals. The following explanation is included to provide the reader with a description of the process.

Each of us, every day of our lives, goes into periods of spontaneous age reenactment. This reliving of past experiences happens every time we respond automatically or behave in a manner not appropriate to a current situation. These responses belong to a former time or place.

Suppose you are reading a novel in which the story line has the hero stranded on a ledge in a remote mountain site, as night is falling and a storm is closing in. The vivid description causes you to react—the back of your neck gets tight, you hold your breath, your hands get sweaty, you want to get away. If you had no memory of desertion, darkness, threatening storms, or being stranded, you could not even imagine the hero's feelings in such a situation. You would have no reaction whatsoever. It is not likely that you were ever in the precise predicaments described in the story, but any one or all of the key elements—alone, stranded, high ledge, night falling, storm approaching—can stir the memory bank in your subconscious mind and cause a defensive reaction.

As you are sitting comfortably by the fire, at home, you logically need no defense reactions—breath holding, chills, sweating, stiff neck, and the like—but these come on automatically. They are a reenactment from your past—a spontaneous age reenactment.

In the course of developing directed age reenactment, I learned, by carefully monitoring patients' defense reactions, how to guide them safely back through the archives of their subconscious minds to the times they first felt threatened and first created particular defense reactions within themselves—and to help them explore the circumstances (initial sensitizing events) that caused those reactions to be fixed in their memory banks. This is possible because the subconscious mind forgets nothing; only the conscious mind forgets. The initial sensitizing event will always have taken place in the first six years of life. In many instances, a patient can go directly to the event, but more likely, he will go backward in time, through a complete file of similar reactions.

The technique of directed age reenactment is straight-forward and makes no use of special hypnotic induction such as imagining pages of the calendar being torn off, deep breathing, or counting backwards. The technique is most effective with persons who have few rigid character traits, because they still retain their unguarded natural inquisitiveness and imagination. It also works with very controlled, rigid persons who unconsciously resist everything by their own questioning, due to their learned fearfulness, but in these cases it takes much more skill and patience on the part of the therapist.

Directed age reenactment is enhanced by the

attendance of five, six, or more people, provided they also want to experience similar reactions within themselves. To a greater or lesser degree, these peripheral participants will identify with and experience the emotions relived by the patient.

A typical directed age reenactment, such as I might conduct with a male patient, for example, proceeds as follows. I sit facing the patient, in a chair equal in height to his. I place one hand on the back of the patient's shoulder or neck and hold the patient's two hands in my second hand. I let my knees rest against the patient's knees. I gently rock the patient in an arrhythmic pattern, which helps the patient disassociate from his immediate surroundings. Then I suggest that the patient close his eyes and ask him to state the first thought that pops into his mind, no matter how inappropriate it may seem.

In this setting, I am in a position to detect the patient's slightest expression of body language, such as tension in the knees, withdrawing of the back, change in breathing, facial expression, tightness of neck muscles, hand sweating, odor of nervousness, restlessness of the feet, and any hesitant, awkward speech, voice inflection, or misplaces modifiers. In a sense, I act as a polygraph detector, but one with many more channels than the standard inanimate machine. As the peripheral participants tune into the patient, they react and, by projecting their feelings of support, strengthen the emotional aura surrounding the patient.

At the outset, I inform the patient that I really don't need to know anything about his past. In a sense, I am only a conduit, storing what I hear in my short-term memory, which will quickly fade. In actual practice, all that is needed to start the process is to detect any body language or voice reaction—or any hesitancy in the patient's response—and to call these reactions to his attention. When I do so, he will instantly react by intensifying and heightening his emotional content (just as we blush more deeply if someone calls attention to our blushing), which will aid in identifying and tracing the source of his reaction.

If the patient is hesitant in his response and starts to draw away, tensing his back muscles, this reaction belongs properly to another time and place; it has nothing to do with the therapist or the present moment. I will ask such questions as, "Who (or what situation) are you drawing away from? What are your feelings right now? Who are you with now? Where do you feel yourself to be? How old are you now?" In general, I try to ask questions that are open-ended. Because the subconscious mind knows only one state of being, the present, I ask each question only in the present tense.

Being completely familiar with the Smith Index and thoroughly experienced in identifying body language, I can age-date each manifestation of the patient's body language. If the patient's feet show an inclination to move or run, I know we are at a two-year-old level (running away). I can ask the patient directly, "As a two-year-old, who do you see yourself running away from? What situation are you running away from?" If the patient doesn't immediately respond, either verbally or physically, my question wasn't relevant, so I change the direction of the inquiry, moving on until I do get an emotional response. Then I again call the patient's reaction to his attention to intensify that reaction and proceed until I can identify the circumstances of its origin.

If the patient is behaving as an infant, I may ask, "Where do you see yourself now? Are you standing? What are you wearing? What time is it, day or night? Are you alone? Describe your crib, the room, the color of curtains (and so forth). Whom do you feel is holding you? What does the touch of your mother feel like? Is your father in this picture? What do your hear him saying? What is the feeling you are getting from your father?"

The real purpose of directed age reenactment is for a patient to return to when and where his emotional reactions first started (initial sensitizing event) and to understand why it was necessary for him to develop these reactions as a means of defense (survival). Once he recalls this event, with all its emotional content, and becomes consciously aware of it, he will never again lose this conscious awareness.

The subconscious mind forgets nothing. The event that is inscribed the deepest is the one with greatest emotional content. When I conduct a directed age reenactment, I create a safe place for the patient to feel free to relive an incident of his early life. During age reenactment, the patient can safely reexperience a family conflict of great stress, complete with innumerable details. The whole family scene can be reconstructed. When the patient reviews all this information and then considers his ten, thirty, fifty, or more years' of experience, he has a chance to revise his perceptions of his family relationships, and to understand his place and importance within his family group.

When working with guarded patients, I pay especial attention to their heightened fears of interpersonal involvement. When I ask a guarded female patient, for example, to tell me what first pops into her head, her answer is, "Nothing does." Because the mind cannot be without thoughts, even for an instant, this indicates a spontaneous age reenactment in itself and tells me that this patient is very fearful of divulging anything about herself. When the feeling of fear comes on strongly, the patient's whole back may become covered with sweat in two to three seconds. Secretiveness is a trait of a child four or five years old; children under four years old tend to be unguarded and effusive. Consequently, the patient's defenses will consist mostly of saying or doing nothing, except for the "right thing," if she can figure out what that is.

Even with guarded patients, there will be flashes of early emotions that inevitably break through. These will only be evident for brief moments, because such patients will tend to withdraw every time they feel exposed. Nevertheless, when these fragments of reenacted memories are put in sharp focus, I am able to guide these patients in and out of reenactment and piece together developmental patterns.

One unique feature of directed age reenactment is that patients are truly in two time frames at once. They are never out of the present nor do they lose any of their adult awareness skills or analytical ability, and at the same time because they feel safe, they are able emotionally to relive their past experiences.

When a patient reenacts the initial sensitizing event behind a particular defense, usually toward the end of a twenty- or thirty-minute session, I have him review his recalled past in all its aspects, using all his present awareness. The chief objective is for the patient to reexperience the full emotions of the event, which will allow him to understand that his response was the only logical response he had available to protect himself at that time in his past. Therapeutically, reviewing the objective circumstances of the event is helpful, but only when patients reexperience all the emotions they first felt and apply all the learning they have acquired since that time can their perceptions change and their fear or anger be released. Only then can their emotional growth resume.

b. Exercise to Reestablish Individuality

The more vulnerable we feel we are, the more we will seek to gain control over all people and situations at hand. When we sense that we are being controlled either by a predicament, another person, or a group of people, the more likely it is that we will become defensive and seek to regain dominance over the situation. While we are actively either on the offense or defense, our bodies' systems are working under stress. In reality, to widely varying degrees, stress is a normal state of existence. However, in the first two years of our lives, in any extreme or prolonged conditions that excessively impact us, the resultant struggle can immediately stifle our emotional growth, and can adversely reduce our drive to express our personal individualities throughout our lives. This exercise is designed to remove early impediments that we have formed and reestablish the sanctity of our individuality in its full form.

After conception and during our formation as special individual fetuses, there was a time when we were free of any outside emotional pressures or influences. Although we were utterly dependent on outside support and protection, we were totally ourselves, with all our potential for ultimate development. In our minds' eyes, through our imagery, we are going to return to that time of our pristine emotional state, that is, when our development was driven solely by the potentials which are encoded in our genetic templates. From this zero point, we will find renewed opportunity to reestablish our faith in our special individualities, that is, to revive belief in ourselves. We will also rework and recycle our attitudes, which will insure the development of personalities that are entirely in accord with the potential patterns that are inscribed in our personal genetic templates.

The whole purpose of this exercise is for us to retrain our subconscious minds so that our deepest feelings and attitudes are revised and reestablished, insuring that our individualities as separate persons are our foremost objectives.

Before we will allow any change in our attitudes, the primary proviso for successful reeducation is feeling safe. All vestiges of fear and defense need to be assuaged. If we feel a need to guard ourselves, we cannot let ourselves change and grow emotionally.

The path of entry into the realm of the

subconscious mind is imagery. To create safe places, we picture in our minds acceptable and comfortable situations. The more vividly and the more often we conjure up the images of these places, the more effective our self-help will be. These personal safe places can be anywhere in the universe that we can be entirely ourselves. We visualize ourselves sitting down, lying on soft grass, or in any situation that is very relaxing. In our personal safe places, away from intruding voices, we are free of any striving to please others, free from any criticism, and pleasantly warm and relaxed. We are totally ourselves. Then, we practice and add to this imagery of our safe places. We use our backgrounds and experiences to enhance our imagery.

Practice image 1:

See a door and a drawer that, because of damp weather, has swelled with moisture, so the drawer and door will no longer open. Now, with prolonged dry weather, picture the door and the drawer working easily, with little or no resistance. In our safe places, the temporary sticking was no problem; it was just an observation. Men in ancient times used the natural phenomenon of swelling of dry wood to split huge slabs of stones, in order to build the pyramids and temples. They would drill a series of holes and fill these by driving very dry wooden pegs to the bottom. Next, they soaked the wooden pegs with water. The dehydrated wood swelled and enlarged to its original size, when it was a green and growing tree. Visualize the tremendous pressure that each formerly dry wooden peg regained, which enabled them to split off huge slabs of rock.

Practice image 2:

See seeds that have spouted. Recall the sprouts that you get at the vegetable stand that you add to your salad and stir-fry. See how pale and fragile they appear. However, their appearance is entirely deceiving. If they are confined in the earth in their early development, they are capable of pushing up through the earth, even forcing their way up through the blacktop of a tarmac. Imagine that when you came into this world your genetic potential and individuality was analogous to that of a sprouting acorn. Imagine that sprouting acorn starting to grow in the ground beneath the tarmac with only the slightest crack above. Like a vigorous acorn sprout, you are able to enter a small crack and grow upward and expand outward. Likewise, intellectually and emotionally, you are naturally growing your individuality outward and upward. The life force in you as an individual is tremendous and can overcome huge resistance. The sprout may seem tender, but you know that it can force its way upward through the earth and expand itself in that crack in the blacktop. Watch it grow as it cracks the black top to become a small sapling. The sprouting potential of our individuality is more than equal to an acorn. Visualize overcoming all efforts of other individuals who attempt to distort your natural emotional development or force you to emulate their own dysfunctional likenesses. You, as the original acorn, now develop into a natural, fully formed, symmetrical oak tree. Your roots are firmly planted in the ground, and you rise up through the resistance of the blacktop and become as individual as a single oak tree. You have overcome all manner of adverse challenges to become a full and emotionally mature personality.

c. Group Anger Management: an Outline

Ideally, the members of our Anger Management Group are in attendance voluntarily, by their own personal choice, and not because some authoritative figure mandated that they need anger therapy. A paying attendee perhaps has even more incentive to grow. From the outset, it is essential for success that those in attendance increasingly perceive that our group provides a safe place to express themselves. Attitude adjustment is the name of the game, but little can be accomplished if participants continue to be guarded or defensive. Reticence and resistance to listening precludes any change in attitude. However, we can expect that most participants at their first session will be wary, so activity should be started with a non-threatening focus. The aim is to engage each member and encourage everyone to participate.

In opening a meeting, we should have an inclusive activity. Some group leaders can share their experiences of hard knocks and thereby engage the group to tell their own stories that will have a common thread of similar experience. In church services, hymn singing has worked for years. In more sophisticated groups, silent individual meditation might be used. Those who have had background in hypnosis can use suggestion with background music to conduct the group through vivid imagery to a protected place. The full attention of relaxed participants is the foundation for success.

Draw on group and individual experience, especially about anger in general. Ask questions.

Ask each participate the same question, such as, *"How has anger worked for you?"* Later, after one or more rounds of responses to each question, when all those who dare have replied, draw a summary of the consensus that all or most attendees could agree upon. Keep a rudimentary log of each respondent's story, so that you can refresh the group's memory in order for all to understand that the follow up questions are pertinent.

Sample questions for the group:

1) Think of your last expressions of strong anger. Explain what you hoped to accomplish with this outburst.

2) What was the effect of your outburst on the other person involved? Were you satisfied with it?

3) Did anger result in accomplishing the

immediate result you hoped for?

4) What has the long-term result of the episode been?

5) How has the long-term effect influenced your continuing relationship with the other person involved?

6) Can you think of any approach or technique, other than anger, that would have achieved the same or better long-term improvement in your relationship?

7) Considering the long-term consequences, is there any other way that you might have behaved that would have provided you with a more satisfying result in interpersonal relationship with this individual?

8) What kind of relationships would you like with various members of your family?

9) Has anger ever improved closeness and love in your family?

10) Rather than exploding with anger, can you offer a suggestion that, in a similar situation in the future, you might use to help yourself? Or do you plan to use anger again in your usual way?

Hopefully, as we get answers, a preponderance of ideas will allow us to select a compilation, which will illustrate that anger is generally used to control and destroy. It will be our aim to use the patients' collective definition of anger and its destructive use so that they will be in general agreement. Tactfully, we can point out to them that they already knew the answer, and that we are merely pointing out what they already basically felt.

Our aim in asking each of these questions is to form a complete definition of anger in all of its ramifications and to demonstrate the stultifying effect that it has on others. Ultimately, we will accept all the agreement we can get and work with this positive definition. The initial group session will be designed to bring our attendees along in their collective intellectual understanding of anger as a concept.

Encourage a discussion concerning the probable triggers for outbreaks of anger in the past and in the future. Identify events of the past that did happen, or should have happened, but did not.

11) How much of the past can you change today?

This can lead to the realization that the past is history and is fixed and final. Anger is for the past. The past may be one second ago or thirty years ago. In the

Middle East, Arabs and Jews have perpetuated anger for two thousand years. The only aspect of any history that is changeable is our attitude and the amount of energy we want to waste on it. A true adult divests all emotional energy from the past, so that he can relate entirely to the present.

12) *What can you do in the future, so the past is not repeated?*

Anger seizes us most of the time with no warning. The exception is when we voluntarily conjure up an image in which we picture ourselves as victims and allege that we have been wronged. If we continue to expand our imaginary scene, we can purposely intensify our anger into rage.

13) *What steps can you take to short circuit the very first part of the anger reaction? How can you recognize anger at the instant of its onset?*

14) *How can you refuse to put energy into it? For instance, if someone calls you a foul or degrading name, do you feel compelled to react?*

15) *Can that name hurt you if you refuse to put energy into it?*

16) *Suppose that vile name is spoken in a completely foreign language by a three-year-old child?*

Should you kill him? Do you always have a choice to respond or not respond to a racial slur? And then, at whom are you logically really angry? Who had the hypersensitive, public access anger buttons?

17) How much do you enjoy the excitement of anger?

18) How much do you enjoy power?

19) How much do you crave the supreme power of unbridled anger or rage?

20) How many and what types of relationships have you wiped out because of your anger?

21) Do you enjoy being around an angry person or a mad vicious dog?

Suggestion to the group:

1) Practice noting every time and place you hear and feel anger from others.

2) Learn all of the permutations of anger and observe how they are used.

3) Make a study and train yourself to instantly identify all the forms of anger. It's like what we did in this country during World War II. Women and physically unfit men volunteered to spend nights and days as airplane spotters for possible raids by German and Japanese aircraft. They took courses and continued studies to enable them to instantly identify the shapes and markings of foreign and U.S. planes in order to give early warning to civil defense. Early spotting of anger is also important, for it, too, can destroy you. With continued practice every day, throughout the day, you will become more and more alert to the early expression of your own anger. You will find that, with real early detection, that is, before your thinking brain is totally shut off, you still have the options of putting energy into anger or letting it pass. It's like a ringing telephone—you can answer it or let it ring, especially if it's someone else's phone. You're making a truly successful life for yourself when no one, not even yourself, forces you to do anything, and you always have options and choices.

The second phase is to let the participants give themselves permission to realize that in the past, when they were small and helpless, they needed anger to sustain themselves, and this protection is no longer needed. Formerly, they had believed that anger was the key to get respect in order to survive. As you listen to the group's adult responses, has that need for each individual been satisfied?

If, on a one-night-stand, our lady friend asks, "Will you respect me in the morning?" what is she really indicating that she wants? She will respect a person who is truly awesome, but what she really wants is acceptance and esteem for who she is.

The challenge to our group is this straightforward:

Do all of you believe that you can and will help another, perhaps lesser, individual who is under attack and needs help?

Believe it or not, the needy person who is under constant attack is you—from within. It is that innermost small child who is so sensitive and hurt that he feels compelled to fight everyone.

Now is the time to seek adjustment in attitude to realize that your original need for respect to maintain your identity is no longer present. You have been successfully maintaining this proof for years. When you were a crying infant in fear of dying, you were angry. The only way you could get attention and respect, and a chance for life, was crying in anger. Even to this day, if nobody will pay respect for your being the true individual that you are, your anger will automatically flare. Then you will force another person to acknowledge your importance in any way you are able. He has ignored your dependency needs and wants. You still use anger to get the attention you feel you must have as a matter of life and death. The irony is that if any person, for whatever reason, can make you angry, in fact, he is in charge of you. He may have to keep his distance, but he is still controlling you. Anger is an infantile way of seeking control and respect.

One way to overcome being a victim and feeling compelled to automatically and instantly defend yourself is to construct images of an infant who was allowed to develop emotionally without this handicap. You do this by understanding, supporting, and nurturing the frightened normal infant that you once were and who is still active in your belief system.

Solicit suggestions from the group on how to visualize such a family constellation wherein an infant could live and feel that he is separate and equally important in his relationship to his parents. When a baby is nurtured in this way, he retains his sense of self-importance. If on the other hand, he is treated as if he is an unwanted, inferior individual, he will maintain himself as a demanding nuisance just to be noticed. The infant adopts this attitude of defense because he feels that he is in such great need most of the time. He reacts to a lack of getting respect, because he senses that he is unwanted as he is, and he feels that he is not truly connected to the family. Therefore, he adopts a deep feeling of shame for who he is and for just being there. However, he repeatedly learns that if he cries with utter frustration and anger, he will get noticed and gain respect and importance.

We can anticipate that the individuals in our group really do not care for human infants, because they themselves were unwanted or poorly tolerated as babies. Consequently, they did not like themselves at that time and are still ashamed of themselves. In some situations, we may find working with animal models, such as kittens or puppies, less threatening. When members of the group are ready to grasp the concept of normal human infants, with their absolute need for support and nurture, we will hopefully be able to help each individual conjure up an imaginary clone of himself, which he can learn to accept. The major obstacle here is that the client will be in denial when we attempt to point out that his current behavior demonstrates that he basically does not like the person he is. Using conventional logic, each individual will boast that all of his fighting has been to prove his worth. Obviously, if you are a black man, you do not have to prove the color of our skin to anyone, especially yourself.

Early on, there probably will be few in the group who will be ready to conceptualize the ultimate in human evolution, which is to totally accept ourselves as we are, developing our potentials to the maximum. Within the individual's current limits, the important initial step is to accept that unappreciated infant who was relatively renounced and disenfranchised by his caretakers during his first year of life:

The whole exercise is to regain that recognition for who you are and only secondarily for what you can do. The very antithesis of this is acting in anger to demand respect from others. You need to feel and accept that you are worthy because you are born as one of God's own creatures.

The technique here is to set up dual themes. We already have the long established one, in which the client defends his self-assumed flawed identity. This is a blatantly false premise, because every animal in this world is born with an attitude already installed; that he has a rightful place as a worthy individual. Currently, the client is acting out by defending this false premise that he is basically a flawed person who deserves little or nothing at all, therefore he must fight for everything.

A treatment model is to set up a parallel situation in which, at its very founding, he was obliged to immediately form his belief concerning his self-worth. At this time, he can readily understand that, as an infant, he would have been totally unable to understand the behavior of adults. An infant is limited to automatic reaction to protect his life and his individuality. At that time, he adopted, and still practices, an attitude about himself and his depreciated self-worth as mandated by his parents. This attitude is that he is very vulnerable and therefore, he must protect himself from every small affront. A normal infant's ultimate defense is anger or aggression to get attention, care, and respect. Today, the need for this attitude is completely gone.

The simple principle here is that if no one liked him when he was young then, in all probability, he did not like himself, because of the characteristics that his caretakers found offensive, even though they were normal. The goal is to create an opportunity for the client to undo the prejudice against accepting infants that he has always maintained. It is no harder than to get him to drop racial prejudice.

The group members were not accepted or tolerated when they were infants themselves. It is reasonable that the very thought that they have an active infant within themselves will not be easily accepted. Therefore, the objective, through the use of imagery, is to, first consciously, and then subconsciously, bring that emotional infant that resides in the innermost part of the client around to where he will be tolerated, liked, and nurtured by this formerly angry individual. He will learn to not only tolerate, but to esteem that infant that he once was. Ask the client if he has ever had the thought or in jest ever said, "The devil made me do it." There is no way he is possessed by the devil, but since early infancy, a fearful inner infant has possessed him. This infant keeps reenacting his deep insecurity—this is his readiness to angrily defend any slight rebuff. Anger at himself is a response to his feelings of inadequacy.

Compared to an adult, an infant has normal foibles and inadequacies deep within himself. We take on stewardship of an infant, a very young kitten, or a pup, not for what they are at that moment, but for the potential they can realize. In fact, starting with imagery of nurturing a small animal may be easier for some to accept than that of a helpless infant.

When you start with the image of a newborn, begin gradually, so as to create some emotional distance and then work into a closer relationship slowly. You approach this newborn with the attitude that you want him to develop in his own individual form to become the best possible person that he is ordained to be. That ultimate form is in the blueprint in his genes.

This is your second chance. Years ago, with only the information they had at that time, your parents did the best they could. Now, you have the information to redo it correctly. From the start, the secret is to treat this infant as a separate and equal individual. You are merely supplying a safe place for him to develop into his own emotional specifications as depicted in his genetic blueprint. Emotional growth is entirely comparable to physical growth, which is simply allowing an arm, a leg, and facial features to grow as designed for a human being.

After a generic infant is accepted, we can approach the concept of an infant who is the exact clone of the patient. Historically, the client has helped others more than he has ever helped himself. Eventually, each can work with a clone of himself. When he can actively synthesize supportive imagery, his subconscious mind, as a passive observer, will accept the image as truth about himself.

The object is not to make this clone into a special individual, but rather provide a safe place to him to grow and develop normally. You merely allow him to flourish under protection, free of rejection. In such a safe place, he will automatically mature into a warm, open, and accepting human. Such a process is like caring for an apple sprout, which, with protective culture, will mature into a tree and produce a bountiful crop of apples.

d. Twelve Steps for Growth

Veterans Independent Enterprises of Washington
Attitude Adjustment Program
(Analogous to the Twelve Step Program)

1) My interpersonal life is failing in fulfillment. I am earnestly and sincerely striving to enhance my understanding and acceptance of myself and other people.

2) I have in the past and still do consider myself to be a victim of people outside of myself, for they seem to hold power over me and determine what I must do and say. My attitude about this will change, for this attitude prevents any favorable adjustment for my future. The conventional cocktail hour has been regarded as an attitude adjustment hour, and it is has blunted my higher moral and behavioral self. Likewise, hard drugs changed my attitude, so that my feelings of insufficiency or worthlessness were temporarily obliterated. My attitude adjustment from now on will be focusing on the truth that I alone am responsible for my behavior.

3) I cannot change anyone else in this world to suit my purposes. I cannot solve any one else's problems. Most of all, I cannot be forced by anyone, especially myself, to change. The only avenue open to me is to clear my head and my belief system of past impediments and allow for my normal emotional growth to supervene.

4) No matter how clever I might have been in the past, I acknowledge that I cannot maneuver anybody else into accepting me.

5) My task is accepting myself. Accepting means that I must allow everyone, including myself, to be as they are at this moment. No amount of force will change anyone. Force will cause people to defend and recede into themselves, but not change.

6) All my beneficial changes will automatically and naturally happen when I relax and stop defending my point of view and my past behavior.

7) The sole reason that I do anything is because I want to. Every explanation by me or anyone else is

after the fact and is a fabrication and an excuse.

8) Anger, except in a very brief period to give extra energy in time of grave danger, or in a limited time to define my territory or add effort to an endeavor, is an infantile device for controlling or destroying another person or thing. The use of anger is the most infantile personality arrest.

9) I am open to listening to suggestions and prudent guidance from support groups, counselors, and especially, from higher spiritual presence. Open mindedness can be threatening, but there can be no change or improvement without it.

10) I can reduce and eliminate stress and prolonged forms of anger, for they are caused by my unrealistic expectations.

11) I am now a fully mature adult and no longer require anyone, even God, to do for me what I can do for myself. I do rejoice and welcome all individuals and groups like Veterans Independent Enterprises of Washington, because they provide me with an

opportunity and a Safe Place for me to restore myself physically and evolve emotionally. Security enables me to attain the personality adjustment that will bring me into compatible and loving relationships with other people.

12) My aim is to relinquish control over myself and others and replace it with prudent management and direction of all talent and energy.

ISBN 141207871-7